www.wadsworth.com

wadsworth.com is the World Wide Web site for Wadsworth and is your direct source to dozens of online resources.

At *wadsworth.com* you can find out about supplements, demonstration software, and student resources. You can also send email to many of our authors and preview new publications and exciting new technologies.

wadsworth.com
Changing the way the world learns ®

The Wadsworth College Success Series

Campbell, *The Power to Learn: Helping Yourself to College Success,* 2nd Ed. (1997). ISBN: 0-534-26352-6

Clason and Beck, *On the Edge of Success* (2003). ISBN: 0-534-56973-0

Corey, *Living and Learning* (1997). ISBN: 0-534-50500-7

Gordon and Minnick, *Foundations: A Reader for New College Students,* 2nd Ed. (2002). ISBN: 0-534-52431-1

Holkeboer and Walker, *Right from the Start: Taking Charge of Your College Success,* 4th Ed. (2003). ISBN: 0-534-59967-2

Petrie and Denson, *A Student Athlete's Guide to College Success: Peak Performance in Class and in Life,* 2nd Ed. (2003). ISBN: 0-534-57000-3

Santrock and Halonen, *Your Guide to College Success: Strategies for Achieving Your Goals,* Media Edition, 2nd Ed. (2002). ISBN: 0-534-57205-7

Van Blerkom, *Orientation to College Learning,* 3rd Ed. (2002). ISBN: 0-534-57269-3

Wahlstrom and Williams, *Learning Success: Being Your Best at College & Life,* Media Edition, 3rd Ed. (2002). ISBN: 0-534-57314-2

The Freshman Year Experience™ Series

Gardner and Jewler, *Your College Experience: Strategies for Success,* Media Edition, 5th Ed. (2003). ISBN: 0-534-59382-8
        Concise Media Edition, 4th Ed. (2001). ISBN: 0-534-55053-3
        The Reader, 5th Ed. (2003). ISBN: 0-534-59985-0
        Expanded Workbook Edition (1997). ISBN: 0-534-51897-4

Study Skills/Critical Thinking

Kurland, *I Know What It Says…What Does It Mean? Critical Skills for Critical Reading* (1995). ISBN: 0-534-24486-6

Longman and Atkinson, *CLASS: College Learning and Study Skills,* 6th Ed. (2002). ISBN: 0-534-56962-5

Longman and Atkinson, *SMART: Study Methods and Reading Techniques,* 2nd Ed. (1999). ISBN: 0-534-54981-0

Smith, Knudsvig, and Walter, *Critical Thinking: Building the Basics,* 2nd Ed. (2003). ISBN: 0-534-59976-1

Sotiriou, *Integrating College Study Skills: Reasoning in Reading, Listening, and Writing,* 6th Ed. (2002). ISBN: 0-534-57297-9

Van Blerkom, *College Study Skills: Becoming a Strategic Learner,* 4th Ed. (2003). ISBN: 0-534-57467-X

Watson, *Learning Skills for College and Life* (2001). ISBN: 0-534-56161-6

Student Assessment Tool

Hallberg, *College Success Factors Index,* http://success.wadsworth.com

50 Ways to Leave Your Lectern

Active Learning Strategies to Engage First-Year Students

Constance Staley
University of Colorado, Colorado Springs

THOMSON

WADSWORTH

Australia • Canada • Mexico • Singapore • Spain
United Kingdom • United States

THOMSON

WADSWORTH

College Success Editor: Annie Mitchell
Assistant Editor: Kirsten Markson
Technology Project Manager: Barry Connolly
Project Manager, Editorial Production: Trudy Brown
Print/Media Buyer: Robert King

Permissions Editor: Joohee Lee
Copy Editor: Ruth Stevens
Cover Designer: Preston Thomas
Compositor: Bruce Saltzman
Text and Cover Printer: Globus Printing Company, Inc.

Printed in the United States of America
1 2 3 4 5 6 7 06 05 04 03 02

For more information about our products, contact us at:
Thomson Learning Academic Resource Center
1-800-423-0563
For permission to use material from this text, contact us by:
Phone: 1-800-730-2214   **Fax:** 1-800-730-2215
Web: http://www.thomsonrights.com

Library of Congress Control Number: 2002100282

ISBN: 0-534-53866-5

Wadsworth/Thomson Learning
10 Davis Drive
Belmont, CA 94002-3098
USA

Asia
Thomson Learning
60 Albert Street, #15-01
Albert Complex
Singapore 189969

Australia
Nelson Thomson Learning
102 Dodds Street
South Melbourne, Victoria 3205
Australia

Canada
Nelson Thomson Learning
1120 Birchmount Road
Toronto, Ontario M1K 5G4
Canada

Europe/Middle East/Africa
Thomson Learning
Berkshire House
168-173 High Holborn
London WC1V 7AA
United Kingdom

Latin America
Thomson Learning
Seneca, 53
Colonia Polanco
11560 Mexico D.F.
Mexico

Spain
Paraninfo Thomson Learning
Calle/Magallanes, 25
28015 Madrid, Spain

Contents

Acknowledgments

The completion of this book means that I owe many thanks to many people: First and foremost to my husband Steve, who split his weekends between fly-fishing on the Middle Fork of the South Platte River and calling me with encouraging words back at the cabin, while I typed away the hours at pine tree-top level in the loft; to my daughters Shannon and Stephanie, who have and continue to enrich my life in far too many ways to list here; to my Mother (and her new husband Ed), who dutifully measured my stress level with each call or visit; to my research assistants Carmen Hernandez and Jaime Garcia, who looked up stacks and stacks of references; to the gifted guest authors and teachers who contributed some of their best discipline-based ideas; to Wadsworth's best—Elana Dolberg, my College Success editor through much of the book's writing, Annie Mitchell, my New College Success editor through much of the book's production, Ilana Sims, my workshop coordinator, and Trudy Brown, my project editor; and to my first-year students, full of energy and wit and enthusiasm, who have learned actively from me—and I from them.

The following activities are from other Wadsworth publications (used with permission):

From *Teaching College Success* (Staley, 1999):
> Group Résumé, These Are a Few of My Favorite Things, If You Could Read My Mind, Graffiti Stations, Trading Places, Wheel in a Wheel, Hollywood (or whatever city you live in) Squares, Spending Time, FYS Course Scorecard, I'm OK; You're...?, An Integrated Education at Work in the Real World, Case Study Exchange, What? So What? Now What?, To Teach Is to Learn Twice, One-Way vs. Two-Way Communication, Visible Quiz, Human Continuum, Listening with a Purpose, Everyone's the Teacher, PowerPoint Twelve-Point Exercise, What's in an A?, Award Ceremony, Autograph Party, Learning Collage, A Letter for Later, You Know What I Really Like About You?

From *Student Success: How to Succeed In College and Still Have Time for Your Friends* (Walter, Siebert, & Smith, 2000):
> Turn a Negative Student-to-Instructor Relationship into a Positive Relationship

About the Author

Constance Staley is Professor of Communication at the University of Colorado, Colorado Springs. She holds a B.S. in education, an M.A. in linguistics, and a Ph.D. in communication. She currently teaches undergraduate communication courses in organizational communication and conflict management, a graduate seminar in training and development, Transition Seminar for transfer students, and she also directs and teaches in the campus's nationally recognized Freshman Seminar Program.

Constance Staley won the University of Colorado, Colorado Springs Outstanding Teacher Award in 1998 and was recently nominated for a CASE U.S. Professor of the Year Award. During 1995 and 1996, Dr. Staley was selected as a Fulbright Scholar to teach in the republic of Kyrgyzstan in the former Soviet Union, representing the University of Colorado and the United States.

While on leave from the University of Colorado from 1988 to 1991, Dr. Staley worked full time for an East Coast Fortune 500 company, where she designed and delivered all management and supervisory training. Her first book, *Communicating in Business and the Professions: The Inside Word* (Wadsworth), was published in 1992. Her most recent work includes the publication of a ten-module faculty training package, *Teaching College Success* (Wadsworth, 1999). Dr. Staley leads regional and on-site workshops for First-Year Seminar faculty from a variety of disciplines and works with institutions across the country to help them develop and refine their First-Year Seminar programs.

"I would like to hear, at least occasionally, 'Teach or Perish'."   *Ernest Boyer*

University of Colorado at Colorado Springs, Spring 2002

Dear Reader:

To be a teacher is to embark on a journey. Looking back, I know I am not the teacher I was twenty-five years ago when I entered the profession—fresh from graduate school, parroting my professors, teaching as I had been taught. Lecture notes in hand, I'd "enter stage left," give my lecture, entertain a few questions, and exit by the same door. This was all I knew and for me then, this was all there was. Now I reflect about how rarely I ventured from the path as I knew it, and I look to the future and wonder how far I have yet to go on this journey. While I have always tried to teach at my best, I have learned a great deal about the process along the way, but I know there is much more to learn.

 I still lecture from time to time in my classes, and in my upper division classes, I lecture for a portion of each class session. However, I realize that auditory learners are in the minority, and that many students learn best by *interacting* or by *doing*. You'll notice that the title of this book is *50 Ways to Leave Your Lectern*—the assumption is you'll come back to it. The title is not *50 Ways to Abandon Your Lectern Forever*. The lecture is a time-honored tradition; it remains the most efficient way to guide students by gathering information from a wide array of resources they may know nothing about. Nevertheless, using a musical analogy, I see myself less as *soloist* or center-stage performer and more as *conductor*, orchestrating and synthesizing a dynamic, multifaceted learning experience. *My teaching is now less about me and more about "them."* The responsibility to learn is theirs; they must pick up their violins and play, not sit idly while I wave my arms wildly as conductor. They don't need me to make music, but I can introduce them to great musical works, composers they've never heard, and beautiful and exotic harmonies. Many of my recent realizations have come from my intense work with college freshmen, but the principles I have developed to

help first-year students learn can be generalized to more intellectually advanced students as well. I have found that these principles of learning apply to all learners.

long my journey, I can point to three milestones that have affected me profoundly and changed my direction: 1) my mid-career, corporate work in training for an East Coast Fortune 100 company while on leave of absence from the university; 2) my experience as a Fulbright Fellow in a remote republic of the former Soviet Union; and 3) my role as Director of the highly successful Freshman Seminar Program at CU-Colorado Springs since 1995.

1. Shortly after earning tenure at CU-Colorado Springs, I requested and was granted a three-year leave of absence. I ventured to the East Coast and took a position with a highly diversified Fortune 100 corporation with annual sales (then) of over nine billion dollars, designing and delivering a major division's supervisory and management training. An excellent professional development opportunity for a mid-career academic, this focused, practical experience taught me a great deal. I learned firsthand about a world many of my students would ultimately enter, about engaging busy, working professionals in the learning process, and about the important intersection between theory and practice in adult education. One of my major responsibilities was working with twenty-five "super-star" managers, whom the company saw as rising talent, for one year of regular, monthly training. Over that period of time, I watched these men and women, many of whom had previously seen training as a "waste of time," look forward eagerly to our sessions together, become inspired "students" despite the pressures of the job, and hone their most critical managerial skills. These managers taught me about the true meaning of active learning; they taught me far more than I taught them. I wrote an ethnography in my head as I worked evenings and weekends to finish my in-progress book on business and professional communication, from the day-to-day perspective of a real-world corporate trainer, and I returned to the classroom more awake and aware than ever before.

2. Three years after I returned from this unusual professional development opportunity in the corporate world, I was chosen competitively as one of then only five Fulbright Fellows in the history of CU-Colorado Springs, and the first and only woman faculty member to be so honored. I joined the faculty of Kyrzyz-American University in Central Asia. This joint venture institution, founded by then Vice President Al Gore and formally opened by Hillary Clinton in 1997, is located in Kyrgyzstan on the Chinese border in the former Soviet Union. In an economy where the average income was $35-50/month, and the transition to a free-market economy was painfully slow and woefully difficult, my students hungered for what I brought them. I taught seven courses during one term and introduced active learning to students whose only experiences had been with the classic European model of education: lectures, followed by memorizing the text word for word and reciting it back to the professor orally in a one-on-one examination session. These Kyrgyz students took a dozen courses each semester, gave standing ovations and thanked me profusely after each class, and consistently requested extra class meetings. Their motivation spurred mine, and I found myself working my hardest to teach at my best. Teaching these students brought unique challenges and taught me a great deal, and the stories I brought back about higher education in the former Soviet Union have broadened the experiences of my students in the United States.

3. The most profound changes I have undergone as a teacher have resulted from teaching and directing our Freshman Seminar Program. Today's freshmen are naïve, inexperienced, often underprepared, and typically apprehensive about the challenges ahead. My fascination with them in the classroom has led me to respond to these new challenges by broadening my research focus as I explore, validate, and write about my experiences as a teacher. My publications have spurred responses from other faculty across the United States, and, in turn, I am continually writing more to help us all cope—and succeed—with our first-year students.

UCLA's Higher Education Research Institute has collected data on our nation's first-year students for thirty-five years, and many of their latest findings are sobering. According to their summaries over the last three years, for example:

1. Academic engagement among our nation's college freshmen has never been lower.
2. A record percentage of first-year students (58 percent) expect at least a **B** average in college.
3. Forty-three percent of freshmen graduated from high school with an A average.
4. Twenty-five percent of first-year expect to work full time while in college.
5. Today's first-year students care less about status and more about affluence.
6. Only 35 percent of first-year students report studying six hours or more per week in the last year.
7. Thirty percent of freshmen report high levels of stress.

We also know that approximately nearly half of first-year students will not persist. They drop out for a variety of reasons: academic difficulty, adjustment difficulties, narrow or uncertain goals, weak or external commitments, financial inadequacies, incongruence (feeling they don't "fit" or "belong"), and feelings of isolation (Tinto, 1996).

The recent Boyer Commission Report (1998) advocates that "The focal point of the first year should be a small seminar taught by experienced faculty . . . with topics that will stimulate and open intellectual horizons and allow opportunities for learning by inquiry in a collaborative environment. Working in small groups will give students not only direct intellectual contact with faculty and with one another, but also give those new to their situations opportunities to find friends and to learn how to be students. Most of all, it should enable a professor to imbue new students with a sense of the excitement of discovery and the opportunities for intellectual growth inherent in the university experience." This, at its best, is what a First-Year Seminar experience is all about. And while the national data are sobering, I respect these students, try to understand the world they live in as young people, and value them as unique, individual learners. My own experience with my first-year students has been more and more positive in recent years, and I believe I have made monumental strides as a teacher in finding innovative ways to help them launch their own college careers.

As Bloom noted many years ago, learning involves three domains: <u>A</u>ffective, <u>B</u>ehavioral, and <u>C</u>ognitive. All three of these domains must be addressed. In our first-year courses, we should not only focus on cognitive development, but also work to encourage positive affect and cultivate particular constructive behaviors. The three domains are more equally weighted than in upper division or graduate courses because of where first-year students are in their development. We must be flexible, and most importantly, we must develop course content with specific ABC goals for students at the forefront.

I assume that you are not reading *50 Ways to Leave Your Lectern* because you wish to explore abstract theories of learning. Rather, I assume your goal is to collect practical ideas for alternative teaching strategies that are immediately applicable in your own classroom. While I have included a theoretical framework to ground the book in Part I, Part II is a collection of useful exercises, divided into seven different types of applications, for you to try. Each exercise has been tested and refined with students at my own and other institutions and with faculty who attended Wadsworth's "50 Ways" workshops across the country between 1999 and 2001. In one chapter, I've included discipline-specific activities, guest-authored by some of the best teachers I know. Some of these authors teach in my own Freshman Seminar Program; others are from other institutions, but they are all known for the impressive work they do with freshmen. I have allowed each author to retain his or her voice, and they have provided you with detailed explanations of some of their most productive activities.

So, thank you for reading and using *50 Ways to Leave Your Lectern*. Parker Palmer (1999) sums it up: "Good teachers possess a capacity for connectedness. They are able to weave a complex web of connections among themselves, their subjects, and their students so that students can learn to weave a world for themselves. The methods used by these weavers vary widely: lectures, Socratic dialogues, laboratory experiments, collaborative problem solving, creative chaos. The connections made by good teachers are not held in their methods but in their hearts... where intellect and emotion and spirit and will converge in the human self." In the end, the activities contained here are merely tools; our skill in using them and our reasons for doing so speak volumes to students. The more you leave your lectern and explore alternative ways to work with your first-year students, the more comfortable you will become taking risks as a teacher, and in turn, the more you will learn from your students. That has been my experience; I hope it is yours as well.

Constance Staley

Constance Staley

Professor of Communication and Director, Freshman Seminar Program
University of Colorado at Colorado Springs

Part I:

- Defining Active Learning

- Using Active Learning in First-Year Classrooms

- Processing Active Learning Experiences:
  Reflection, Application, Integration

- Designing Active Learning Experiences

- Assessing Active Learning Experiences

Defining Active Learning

From time to time in higher education, a new word or phrase enters our collective lexicon. *Active learning* is such a phrase. Many of us use the term, most of us think we understand it—even though our views may differ sharply from those of a colleague—and all of us believe we create it in our classrooms. But if we were to query the collection of students on the other side of the lectern, I wonder if we would be surprised at their responses. What is active learning and how do we get there from here—wherever *there* and *here* are for us as individual faculty? And, we should definitely ask, why is active learning important in today's college classroom?

According to Meyers and Jones (1993):

A subtle but important change is taking place in American higher education. Teachers are beginning to talk with each other about teaching and, as a result, to change the ways they teach. Though hardly a revolution, this conversation about teaching breaks a long tradition reflecting an almost feudal mentality in which teachers surrounded their classrooms with psychological moats and fortifications. The lords and ladies of academe seldom discussed what went on within their castles. And, when the teaching nobility did meet, their conversations revolved around research and discipline-related issues—not teaching. Happily, signs indicate a changing perspective. (p. 3)

Unless our institutions have active "teaching circles," well-constructed peer-review systems, or interdisciplinary team-taught courses, few of us are ever quite sure what goes on in other faculty members' classrooms. We are on our own; we work to create a learning environment based on how we have taught before or how we were taught ourselves.

There is no doubt about it: our profession is changing to meet changing times and changing students. For years, aphorisms about teaching have been plentiful (Elmore, 1991; Weimer, 1990): "If you know it, you can teach it." "Faculty teach content." "Professors are hired to PROFESS, not really teach." "The higher the level of education, the more students should WANT to master the subject." "The ability to teach well is a gift that descends from heaven on the shoulders of a chosen few." "Differences in the quality of teaching are merely a matter of taste or style."

In higher education today, however, we have begun to question these myths and to dispel them. There is greater emphasis on quality teaching and how to achieve it: "If there are born teachers, there are born physicians, born attorneys, and born engineers. Yet those who are naturally great at these professions invariably spend an unnatural amount of

3

time acquiring skills and practicing in the vortex of intense competition. Potentially great teachers become great teachers by the same route" (Seldin, 1995, p. 1). As teachers, many of us strive for continuous improvement, never satisfied that we have learned all there is to know about the challenges of engaging students. John Dewey (1933) once said, "Teaching can be compared to selling commodities. No one can sell unless someone buys. . . [yet] there are teachers who think they have done a good day's teaching irrespective of what pupils have learned" (p. 35). Today's faculty are more mindful of the reciprocal relationship between teaching and learning.

Academic journals now center on teaching excellence *(Journal on Excellence in College Teaching, New Directions for Higher Education, College Teaching*, and *Innovative Higher Education*, for example), and numerous books have been written on the subject (for example, Davis, B. G., 1993; McKeachie, 2002; Seldin, 1995, Weimer, 1990). Seminal writings by influential educators are prompting this paradigmatic shift from *teaching* to *learning*:

> A paradigm shift is taking hold in American higher education. In its briefest form, the paradigm that has governed our colleges is this: A college is an institution that exists *to provide instruction*. Subtly but profoundly we are shifting to a new paradigm: A college is an institution that exists *to produce learning*. This shift changes everything. It is both needed and wanted. (Barr & Tagg, 1995, p. 13)

As today's college teachers, we are encouraged to see ourselves not as "Sage on the Stage," but rather as "Guide on the Side" (King, 1993), facilitating a multifaceted learning experience—an approach that requires a shift of *attention*, a sharing of *control*, and a need for different *communication skills*. Attention is shifted from the teacher exclusively to both teacher *and* students, control is shared among all as the level of participation increases, and communication skills center on *facilitation*, rather than primarily *oration*.

Often, we assumed that if students simply sat in our classes, they would learn to think critically, write creatively, and speak competently. Active learning, on the other hand, has two underlying assumptions: 1) that learning is not accidental or automatic, and 2) that different people learn in different ways. The corollaries to these two assumptions are that students learn best by applying subject matter—learning by doing—and that teachers who use only one teaching approach lose significant numbers of students (Meyers & Jones, 1993). Now we use classification systems to help students and teachers understand learning preferences, such the Myers-Briggs Type Indicator (MBTI), or the Kolb Learning Style Model, or we talk of Multiple Intelligences, Right-Left Brain Differences, and a host of other systemizations. We understand that "learning is not so much an additive process, with new learning simply piling up on top of existing knowledge, as it is an active, dynamic process in which the connections are constantly changing and the structure reformatted" (Cross, 1991, p. 9). Powerful learning can result when all five senses are engaged (Marchese, 2001).

More than simply a set of techniques, active learning is partly an *attitude* held by both students and faculty that works to make learning effective. It is, "in short, any learning activity engaged in by students in a classroom other than listening passively to an instructor's lecture" (Faust & Paulson, 1998). In many ways, a focused effort to engage students at the undergraduate level is, in essence, an attempt to make the undergraduate experience more like the graduate experience, where students engage, think critically, discuss, and problem solve as a natural and expected part of the learning experience. Why not "front load" the educational experience with this type of intellectual immersion, rather than reserve it for students late in their college careers?

Why this "sudden" interest in engaging students as active learners? Many catalytic factors have converged to generate an increased focus on student learning (Staley, 1999):

1. Educational spokespersons at all levels are advocating the need for quality teaching in the classrooms of America.

2. Parents of college students are demanding more for their tuition dollars.

3. Attrition levels warrant a look at why students are leaving our nation's colleges and universities in high numbers.

4. Many institutions of higher education are reevaluating the importance of good teaching and considering changing faculty reward systems correspondingly.

5. Teaching with technology (distance learning and "smart" classrooms) is requiring faculty to reevaluate not only what they teach, but how and why they teach it.

6. Employers increasingly criticize graduates' underdeveloped "real-world" skills and lack of readiness for the workforce.

7. A movement to assess student learning is sweeping our colleges and universities.

States, for example, now receive nationally publicized "report cards" on six variables relating to higher education:

1. Preparation—How well are students in each state prepared to take advantage of college?
2. Participation—Do state residents have sufficient opportunities to enroll in college-level programs?
3. Affordability—How affordable is higher education for students and families in each state?
4. Completion—Do those who enroll make progress toward and complete their certificates and degrees in a timely manner?

5. Benefits—What economic and civic benefits do each state receive from the education of its residents?

6. Learning—What do we know about student learning as a result of education and training beyond high school?

Interestingly, *Measuring Up 2000* awarded all states grades on the first five variables relating to higher education, but no state received a grade on the sixth: learning. Instead, each state received an "incomplete." According to Peter Ewell, one of the nation's foremost authorities on outcomes assessment, "Fewer than ten states administer a common test to large numbers of college students—and these states do so for different reasons. . . . Such variations in scope and purpose mean that states employ very different methods when they assess college students, if they do so at all" (Ewell, 2000). Patrick Callan, President of the National Center for Public Policy and Higher Education, the group that conducted the *Measuring Up 2000* study, admits "As an educator, it's an embarrassment that we can tell people almost anything about education except how well students are learning" (Abel, 2000).

Or consider the disturbing findings generated by a national survey of more than 1300 chief academic officers by the National Center for Postsecondary Improvement. Results of this extensive survey indicated that the assessment movement during the past 15 years has had little major impact on one of its major goals—improving student learning. They report that institutions have not made much use of assessment data for academic decision-making and resource allocation (Cuseo, 2001).

Just what *do* we know about student learning? Looking back,

Educators have never had the scientist's freedom to patiently wait for the research technology to catch up with their curiosity. Every year, a new batch of students arrives at the school door, whether we understand how their brains develop or not. We have had to find a way to bypass students' brains in order to carry out our professional assignment. . . . We also didn't understand the other underlying mechanisms that govern significant teaching and learning concerns, such as emotion, interest, attention, thinking, memory, and skill development. . . . Deep down, we could never be sure if students learned because of our efforts, or despite them. (Sylwester, 1995, pp. 2–3)

Fortunately today, cognitive science, the psychology of motivation and affect, and student development studies have become fertile research emphases, resulting in promising findings with the capacity to change how we teach. Current thinking about learning includes the following premises (Ewell, 1997):

1. The learner is not a "receptacle" of knowledge, but rather creates his or her learning actively and uniquely.

2. Learning is about making meaning for each individual learner by establishing and reworking patterns, relationships, and connections.

3. Every student learns all the time, both with us and despite us.

4. Direct experience decisively shapes individual understanding.

5. Learning occurs best in the context of a compelling "presenting problem."

6. Beyond stimulation, learning requires reflection.

7. Learning occurs best in a cultural context that provides both enjoyable interaction and substantial personal support.

Today, college teachers must know much more than their disciplines:

> Teaching in the college classroom is becoming increasingly complicated. It is no longer sufficient for the college professor to be competent in a field of specialty and to "profess" a substantial base of knowledge to a classroom full of willing students. Today's effective college teachers must be prepared not only to share in-depth knowledge of their discipline but also to know something about college students and how they learn. Faculty are also expected to cultivate skills in different methods of teaching and assessment—areas in which they have had little or no preparation. (Sutherland & Bonwell, 1996, p. 3)

Recently, many teacher/scholars have begun to tackle the questions of what we can do to facilitate student learning. Chickering and Gamson's now classic work (1987, 1991) identifies seven principles for good practice in undergraduate education. They suggest that we as teachers:

1. encourage student/faculty contact.

2. encourage cooperation among students.

3. encourage active learning.

4. give prompt feedback.

5. emphasize time on task.

6. communicate high expectations.

7. respect diverse talents and ways of learning.

Peter Ewell (1997) suggests that teachers use:

1. approaches that emphasize application and experience.

2. approaches in which faculty constructively model the learning process.

3. approaches that emphasize linking established concepts to new situations.

4. approaches that emphasize interpersonal collaboration.

5. approaches that emphasize rich and frequent feedback on performance.

6. curricula that consistently develop a limited set of clearly identified, cross-disciplinary skills that are publicly held to be important.

While suggestions such as these make sense, and they have proven their effectiveness through our own experience, the issue of quality teaching becomes even more challenging when the students in question are veritable newcomers to the college scene. First-year students, in particular, may be eager about their new venture, but many are not necessarily sophisticated gourmet diners at the "learning table." A five-star meal (or lecture) that begins with escargot and ends with Crepes Suzette could be intimidating, and its subtle tastes easily lost on inexperienced palates. Leamnson (1999) uses a similar analogy:

> In the case of the pianist, someone in the audience who had heard the music many times, had perhaps played it herself, would experience something quite different from the first-time listener. New college students in a classroom are somewhat like the musically inexperienced at their first concert. Treated to a virtuoso teaching performance, the student response might be a great sense of awe—important, but well short of what is needed for learning to occur. (p. 17)

Using Active Learning in First-Year Classrooms

> "All educators should spend some time with a one-year-old child whose day revolves around learning. Every new encounter is an adventure; every new idea a revelation. One-year-olds learn through exploration and experimentation. They feel, taste, shake, drop, smell, and examine carefully everything in their world. Once they are familiar with the object, they turn it upside down and explore it all over again. Small children find joy in the process of exploration. They are the quintessential active learners. What has happened to these active learners by the time they get to our institutions? When did our students stop being excited about the process of learning? When and why did learning cease to be a 'hands-on' activity?" (Brown & Ellison, in Hatfield, 1995, p. 39)

In 1858, John Henry Cardinal Newman wrote *The Idea of a University*: "an alma mater, knowing her children one by one, not a foundry, or a mint, or a treadmill" (p. 165). Today some might wonder whether his idea (or *ideal*) is dead and gone. We are told that "higher education is not as central to the lives of today's undergraduates as it was to previous generations. Increasingly, college is just one of a multiplicity of activities in which they are engaged every day. For many, it is not even the most important of these." (Levine & Cureton, 1998, p. 14).

What are today's students like?   First of all, 63 percent of high school graduates go on to college today, compared to 49 percent twenty years ago (McGrath, 2001).   The mandate for higher education has changed: to educate as many citizens as possible.   The Boyer Commission writes in its *Reinventing Undergraduate Education*:

> In a great many ways the higher education system of the United States is the most remarkable in the world. The speed with which it developed, its record of achievement, the extent of its reach, the range of its offerings are without parallel. And, particularly in the years since World War II, the system has reached a higher proportion of the national population than that of any other country... we are, as a country, attempting to create an educated population on a scale never known before. (1998, An Overview)

While this broad-based, national goal gives us the most highly educated citizenry in the world, it also changes the dynamics within individual classrooms. Most of us who have watched students come and go over the years have an intuitive feel for today's students and their characteristics based on experience and observation; the published reviews, on the other hand, are mixed.   In a recent issue of *About Campus* (2000), Newton begins,

> Students entering college at the beginning of this new century are a distinctive generation. Labeled millennials, Internet gens, generation Y, and baby boomers II, they have been described as ambitious, precocious, stressed, indifferent, wayward, techno-nerd, heterogeneous, politically conservative, and sexually active. These descriptions are only a portion of many qualities that make up the complex mosaic that is this generation. (p. 8)

While standardized test scores, such as the ACT, have held steady in recent years (ACT, 2002), institutions report that students are coming to college more overwhelmed and damaged than in the past with rising percentages of eating disorders, classroom disruption, drug and alcohol abuse, gambling, and suicide attempts (Levine & Cureton, 1998). Faculty complaints about disruptive students are on the rise, and nearly one-third of undergraduates report having taken a basic skills or remedial course in reading, writing, or math. Past issues in the *Chronicle of Higher Education* report such potentially troubling headlines as: "University to offer big tuition discounts for joining clubs or attending events," "Insubordination and intimidation signal the end of decorum in many classrooms," "One in 11 freshmen reports having a disability," "Freshmen men select Adam Sandler as the person they would most like to be; women select 'Mom,'" "Freshmen say biggest event of their lives was losing virginity," and "Study documents the extent of students' credit-card debt." According to a more recent *Chronicle* article, some problems appear to intensify during the freshmen year: "Freshmen pay, mentally and physically, as they adjust to life in college" (Bartlett, 2002).

Gonzales and Lopez (2001) worked with faculty to categorize six different types of "problem student": disengaged, disinterested, disrespectful, disruptive, defiant, and disturbed. Create and enforce behavioral standards in the classroom, they suggest, and in keeping with the philosophy espoused here, examine your teaching style: "Classroom practices that create an active learning environment will increase student engagement and interest and thus should reduce disengagement and disinterest." Students at all types of colleges and universities are assigned less reading and are reading less than ten years ago (Kuh, 1999). The National Survey of Student Engagement (NSSE) conducted by researchers at Indiana University reported that 55 percent of students spend only one hour or less outside of class studying for each hour in class, as opposed to the recommended three hours (College Study Habits). According to Astin (1993), "Hours spent studying is positively related to almost all academic outcomes. . . . Hours per week spent attending classes or labs has many fewer associations with student outcomes. . ."

Other reports are more optimistic. Howe and Strauss (Lowery, 2001) see today's up-and-coming generation as precisely that: up and coming. In their book, *Millennials Rising: The Next Great Generation* (2000; also see http://www.millennialsrising.com), they point to lower rates of school killings, renewed closeness to parents, a team versus individual orientation, and a sense of optimism among youth born between 1982 and the present. "By the end of this decade," they conclude, "Millennials may well transform the American campus as much as Boomers did in the sixties, but they will transform it in the opposite direction" (p. 11). The opposition disagrees: "At heart," Levine and Cureton report (1998), "undergraduates are worried about whether we can make it as a society, and whether they can actually make it personally" (p. 51).

Newton's (2000) compilation takes a more evenhanded view, recognizing that any generation of students has its strengths and weaknesses.

MORE:	LESS:
✓ grown-up, "home alone," indulged	✓ emotionally mature
✓ group-oriented, likely to have brief encounters	✓ coupled
✓ technologically proficient than their parents, teachers, and bosses	✓ experienced in the discipline required for in-depth study
✓ likely to work full or part-time	✓ willing to sacrifice for a goal
✓ stressed and anxious	✓ focused
✓ ambitious	✓ realistic about what it takes
✓ rule-conscious	✓ interested in following rules

These descriptions pertain to college students in general. What can we say about first-year students in particular? UCLA's Higher Education Research Institute (HERI), "Home of the CIRP: The nation's oldest and largest study of higher education for over three decades" [see http://www.gseis.ucla.edu/heri/heri.html], focuses primarily on describing the nation's freshman class each year. The CIRP (Cooperative Institutional Research Program) Freshman Survey is the most widely used source of information about college and college students in the nation. Since the survey's inception in 1966, more than 10 million students at more than 1,500 institutions have participated. Last year's press release entitled "College Freshmen More Politically Liberal Than in the Past, UCLA Survey Reveals" reported other trends as well:

1. "Renewed Interest in Politics and Activism"

Compared to last year's record low of 28.1 percent, 31.4 percent of incoming freshmen consider it essential for them to keep up-to-date with political affairs—perhaps due to the controversy surrounding the 2000 contested presidential election—nevertheless representing the largest one-year increase since the presidential election in 1972.

2. "Interracial Interaction Hits Record High"

Seventy percent of incoming freshmen reported having socialized with individuals from another ethnic group within the last year.

3. "Sense of Health and Wellness Hits Record Low"

Representing a steady downward trend, self-ratings of physical and emotional health for freshmen hit record lows.

4. "Record Number Report No Religious Preference"

A record number of freshmen, 15.8 percent, reported no religious preference with accompanying declines in the percentage of freshmen who pray or meditate once a week or more.

5. "Record Levels of Academic Disengagement, Record High Grades"

In another steady downward trend, record numbers of freshmen report feeling frequently bored in class (41.1 percent), with only 34.9 percent reporting that they studied or did homework six or more hours per week in the last year. However, high school grades continue to climb with 44.1 percent of freshmen reporting "A" averages in high school.

In recent years' HERI reports, the issue of academic disengagement has been a noticeable and disturbing trend. According to Mediascope (2000), "Americans spend an average of 9½ hours each day watching television, going to movies, renting videos, reading magazines, listening to music, or surfing the Web." The pace of society has quickened, and as is the case with the rest of us, many pursuits compete for college students' attention. Students today are often exceptionally good at multitasking (listening to music, watching a DVD, surfing the Net, and doing homework all at the same time)—the ability to be broadly attentive (a skill set needed by a successful corporate CEO). However, the result is that their focus is more "shotgun" than "rifle," their learning is more surface than deep, and their studies often ease down to the bottom of a long "to do" list.

A particularly important issue relating to first-year students is the centrality of affect and motivation to learning. The challenge is not simply to amass and organize information to transfer to students; it is to inspire them to become emotionally involved—or engaged—in the content. Learning is a process that can be "externally encouraged, but only internally initiated" (Leamnson, 1999). How can we fully engage first-year students in the learning process?

Consider the following analogy: I am a self-avowed, unabashed car fanatic. I love to read about cars, compare cars, shop for cars, and drive cars. As a young person, my father spent hours with me talking about the innovations of each year's new models, comparing the Chevy with the Ford or the Honda with the Toyota, and test-driving new models just for fun. My friends all ask for my advice when they are in the market for a new car, and my husband always asks me to identify unfamiliar models as we spot them on the freeway. Cars are one of my passions, and I am eager to learn everything I possibly can about them. No one ever has to coax me into taking part in a conversation about cars or cajole me into reading the most recent edition of *Car and Driver* or *Track and Field*.

We all have such passions, including those we hold deeply about the fascinating disciplines we have chosen to pursue. The question is: How do we capture and recreate the passion we hold for biology, or literature, or mathematics in our students? Leamnson (2000) writes,

> Most teachers would agree that if their students were ever to become as "involved" with history, chemistry, or economics as they are in movie stars, rock musicians, and computer games, teaching would become effortless. . . . But most teachers would like their students to become involved with a subject for the same reasons they are—because the subject has an inner structure that is intrinsically ordered, explanatory, or even beautiful. But we must be honest here, and admit that the attractiveness of our discipline came at a price. No one is born with a cognitive interest in anything. (p. 39)

How can we effectively pass on the passion we hold for intellectual inquiry? The emotional, affective components of learning are central to a response to this question (Caine & Caine, 1991):

1. Social interactions and emotional well-being are a) critical to our survival and b) deeply motivating.
2. Learning is as natural as breathing, but it can be either facilitated or inhibited.
3. The search for meaning occurs through patterning; emotions are critical to patterning.
4. The optimal state of mind for learning is high challenge and low threat—*relaxed alertness*.
5. Acquiring new knowledge fundamentally changes the way the self is organized.

Beyond these tenets, we also know that "a particularly powerful stimulus for setting students' emotional barometers are teachers themselves. The old observation that students tend to like a subject if they like the teacher has, then, a real basis in the biology of learning. Making teaching and learning a more personal interaction between teacher and students might well be an effective first step in getting students themselves hooked on a subject" (Leamnson, 2000, p. 40). Ellis (2000) found that teacher confirmation plays a significant role in students' cognitive and affective learning. Teacher confirmation, she reported, is best represented by a three-factor solution: a) teachers' response to students' questions-comments, b) demonstrated interest in students and their learning, and c) teaching style.

Years ago, Bloom (1956, 1976) recognized that as teachers, we have goals in three different domains: affective, behavioral, and cognitive. If we are teaching a course in chemistry, we want students to 1) like the subject, enjoy the course, feel positively about pursuing the discipline (affective goals), b) develop productive behaviors, such as safety habits in the laboratory, timeliness in completing assignments (behavioral goals), and c) learn the content of the course (cognitive goals). Cognitive goals are where most faculty center their attention; however, with first-year students, particularly today, the emphases may need to be more equally weighted. In today's first-year classrooms, instructors must work to motivate, engage, and support students.

Cognitive goals, the position to which most of us gravitate as faculty, are typically pursued through lecture as the delivery mode of choice. Although lecturing is efficient, it is less effective with today's students, particularly first-year students. Through research (Staley, 1999), we know that:

⇒ Most teachers speak at 100-200 words per minute; most students can listen attentively to about 50-100 words per minute, or about half of what is being said (Silberman, 1996).

⇒ Students retain 70 percent of the first ten minutes of lecture, but only 20 percent of the last ten minutes (McKeachie, 1986).

⇒ In one study, students finishing a lecture-style introductory psychology course knew only 8 percent more than a control group of students who had never taken the course (Rickard, Rogers, Ellis, & Beidleman, 1988).

⇒ Lecturing is most effective with auditory learners. It assumes that all students have similar learning styles and identical informational needs. A 1986 study by the University of Minnesota and 3M Corporation found adding visuals to presentations increased persuasiveness by 43 percent, comprehension by 8.5 percent, retention by 10.1 percent, and attention by 7.5 percent (Shaluta, 2000).

⇒ Up to 40 percent less time is required to present information when a visual is used to increase comprehension. A picture is worth not only 1000 words, but it is three times more effective than are words alone (Silberman, 1996).

⇒ Like a computer, the human brain needs to be "on" in order to work. It cannot retain information without "saving" or processing it by actively linking new concepts to existing knowledge (Silberman, 1996).

⇒ No matter how learning styles are assessed (the Myers-Briggs Type Indicator, Neurolinguistic Programming, Kolb's Learning Style Inventory, etc.), students come in all "shapes and sizes" as learners. However, a general mismatch of teaching versus learning styles exists at the college level. For example, a study of over 2000 faculty and 27,000 students indicates that on the MBTI, three times as many students are "sensing" "perceivers" as their professors, and almost twice as many faculty are "introverted" "intuitors" than their students (DiTiberio & Hammer, 1993). As subject matter experts, faculty know *what* students should learn in a particular course, but they may not assess how they are teaching, that is, by using their own learning preferences or the style they were forced to use when they were students themselves. *Audience analysis* is as important a concept for college faculty as it is for professional public speakers or political candidates running for office.

⇒ Students face *preoccupations, pressures*, and *priorities* that make listening to an extended lecture difficult (Staley & Staley, 1992). Instead of listening to your lecture, they may well be thinking about the midterm they must take later in the day (for which they may not be prepared), the "all-nighter" they'll have to pull to finish the research paper due in tomorrow's eight o'clock class, or the argument they had earlier in the day with their significant other. In an innovative experiment reported some years ago in the *San Francisco Sunday Examiner and Chronicle*, a psychology instructor shot off a gun at random intervals during a lecture and asked students to record their thoughts at each moment the gun sounded. He found his worst fears as a lecturer were confirmed: 20 percent of the students were pursuing erotic thoughts; 20 percent were reminiscing about something; 20 percent were actually paying attention to the lecture; 12 percent were actively listening. The others were worrying, daydreaming, thinking about lunch or, interestingly, religion (8 percent) (Adler & Towne, 1987, p. 235).

What does the relatively recent, gradually amassing research on active learning say? How effective is it? Do active learning techniques make a difference in student motivation and learning? DeNeve and Heppner (1997) found mixed results in 175 studies, only 12 of which directly compared active and passive learning. Their own study concluded: "Active learning techniques are more effective for achieving some goals, while lectures are more effective for achieving other goals" (p. 243).

McCarthy and Anderson (2000) compared the results of teacher-centered discussion to role-playing and collaborative activities in both history and political science classes. They report:

> Our results indicate that using certain active learning techniques may well enable students to absorb and retain information just as well as, if not better than, the more traditional methods. The role-playing history students participated more in class *and* did better on the exam by nearly a whole letter grade than their peers engaged in teacher-centered discussions. This is even more significant when one considers that the group role-play students assumed the role of only one historical group. Despite writing about four different groups on the subsequent exam— presumably three that they did not even "play" in class—they still did better. The political science students who participated in the opinion poll activity also performed better on a brief essay quiz than students taught the same material in a lecture format. Moreover, both activities were efficient; they consumed the same amount of classroom time as their traditional alternatives. (pp. 290–291)

Lindquist (1997) conducted an experiment contrasting traditional lecture (passive) and cooperative (active) learning using university faculty as subjects. Faculty perceived that cooperative learning contributed to classroom goodwill, perceived achievement, and actual achievement. Faculty also scored significantly higher on examinations following the active, versus the passive, learning activity.

In a study of students in an introductory economics lab, students overwhelmingly rated that a collaborative learning lab was very worthwhile and that working in groups (as opposed to individually) was more enjoyable and helpful (Moore, 1998). Livengood (1992) found that psychological variables (effort/ability reasoning, goal choice, and confidence) are strongly associated with the variables of academic success as measured by participation and satisfaction. When properly used, active learning enhances motivation to learn, the ability to retain knowledge, depth of understanding, and appreciation of the subject matter (Felder & Brent, 1996). Teaching and learning become a collaborative process; learning draws on the naturally diverse experiences of students with regard to gender, cultural diversity, age, etc.; students are prepared to become lifelong learners; and "simultaneity" makes learning more interesting (Kagan, 1992). Instead of calling on one student at a time in a sequential manner, half the students involved in a group activity, for example, may be talking at once.

Recent studies of classroom participation have uncovered mixed results. Fassinger (1997) found that the traits of individual students and the class as a whole are more strongly correlated with student interaction than are specific instructor behaviors. Others, however, have concluded that some instructor actions do contribute to affecting student interaction (Auster & MacRone, 1994; Howard, Short, & Clark, 1996; Nunn, 1996).

Reynolds and Nunn (1998) found that students participate more and experience less fear in First-Year Seminar classes, and are more satisfied with their amount of participation. Among First-Year Seminar students, first-year students in general, female students, and students expecting to receive an A are more likely to view instructors' teaching techniques as affecting their participation than are other student groups.

Recent studies have also begun to explore the role of classroom academic experiences on students' decisions to leave college (Nora, Cabrara, Hagedorn, & Pascarella, 1996), the relationship between developing a sense of belonging and discussing course materials outside of class (Hurtado & Carter, 1997), and cooperative learning as it relates to departure decisions (Tinto, 1997). Braxton, Milem, Sullivan, and Shaw (2000) investigated the relationship between active learning and student departure and found that "faculty classroom behaviors play a role in the student departure process." In their study, three of four indices of active learning had a statistically significant influence on one or more of the study's central constructs: students' social integration, commitment to the institution, and intent to return.

In a study to explore an increase in Chickering and Gamson's seven process indicators for good practice in higher education between 1990 and 1994, Kuh and Vesper (1997) focused on institutional, rather than individual classroom, practices. They found slightly greater exposure to good practice at baccalaureate institutions, although the change was statistically significant for only one indicator (faculty-student interaction). Little change was seen at doctoral-granting institutions. As for other indicators, they report, "it is somewhat disappointing that experiences with peer cooperation and active learning did not increase at these institutions, given the burgeoning literature on their relationship to student learning" (p. 52). In another study, Kuh, Pace, and Vesper (1997) found that active learning and cooperation (in that order) among first- and second-year students were the best predictors of gains for both women and men at three types of institutions.

If the evidence is in fact beginning to mount, why is it so challenging for faculty to make the transition to active learning, as many of us will admit? A primary reason may be that "Little has been done to translate the research on cognition and learning 'into directly applicable information relevant to...classroom practice'" (Meyers & Jones, 1993; Pintrich, 1988, p. 72). The objections to active learning are often actively debated among faculty (Felder & Brent, 1996; Millis & Cottell, 1998; Staley, 1999):

1. If I spend class time on active learning activities, I'll never get through the syllabus.

The most common objection to active learning among college faculty centers on coverage: active learning sacrifices valuable content for time-consuming activities. Increasingly, however, research indicates that students learn and retain more when they are actively engaged. Faust and Paulson (1998) write: "weighing content coverage against active learning creates a devil's bargain: Either teach more material and have students learn less, or teach less material and have students learn more of it" (p. 17). While the second alternative may be unpalatable to some, the first makes no sense at all. Active learning activities may be blended with other teaching methods to find the productive mix with which we are comfortable as individual instructors. Faculty who remain partial to the lecture as a teaching method should think of active learning activities as ways to *enhance, extend, and apply* the lecture before, during, or afterward.

2. If I don't lecture, I'll lose control of the class.

Faculty worry that too much student interaction will lead to pandemonium. True, the noise level is typically higher in a class in which students are engaged and involved, but it is possible to set ground rules in advance, to pace classroom activities so that quiet times alternate with noisy ones, and to become accustomed to the "messiness" of engagement and see it as a sign that learning is taking place. Students involved in activities or discussion are typically more engaged in learning than are students daydreaming through a lecture.

3. My students will complain; they expect to be *taught*.

Felder and Brent (1996) warn:

> It's not that student-centered instruction doesn't work when done correctly—it does, as both the literature and our personal experience in two strikingly different disciplines richly attest. The problem is that although the promised benefits are real, they are neither immediate nor automatic. The students, whose teachers have been telling them everything they needed to know from the first grade on, don't necessarily appreciate having this support suddenly withdrawn. Some students view the approach as a threat or as some kind of game, and a few may become sullen or hostile when the find they have no choice about playing. (p. 43).

It is true that active learning puts more responsibility on the learner. If instructors are not simply going to lecture over the text chapter, week after week, students who want to perform well will need to read and study on their own. An active learning approach in the classroom must be "sold" to students up front in a course, and its far-reaching benefits pointed out. Well-designed interactive experiences lead to stronger interpersonal relationships, less absenteeism, more personal responsibility, higher motivation, and a variety of other positive outcomes.

4. My colleagues will lose respect. They'll think I'm spending valuable class time on *fun and games*.

Faculty who try active learning techniques should be responsible for communicating their efforts and educating their colleagues. Give a brown-bag seminar on campus, publicize your methods to other faculty, and spread the word about positive results.

5. **I don't have time to rework my courses. I'm already overloaded with too much to do.**

It's true that each time one develops or revamps a course—putting lecture highlights on PowerPoint slides, for example—a significant investment of time is required. However, once the course enhancements have been completed, they may be reused in subsequent terms, and items generated for one course may be applicable to other courses, as well.

6. **Active learning is "soft"; I'll have to sacrifice rigorous standards**.

The research in this field consistently demonstrates that well-constructed groupwork, projects, service learning, and a host of other active learning techniques actually raise student achievement.

7. **Normal assessment techniques won't work. How will I gauge how my students are doing?**

Evaluation must be placed into a broader context: Do we typically evaluate students' attentiveness during lectures? Active learning can increase students' accountability.

8. **The traditional model worked in the past.**

Models of the past may not necessarily be as appropriate today; in fact, they may have been less effective than we actually remember. There is a growing sense among faculty that the "old ways" do not work as well as they used to. Further, new research about the learning styles of today's students signifies a need for change.

Processing Active Learning Experiences: Application, Reflection, Integration
"To help students translate knowledge into action, we must examine the ways in which
what we know may not always be congruent with what we do." (Komives, 2000)

In my upper-division conflict management course, I devote one three-hour class session to a labor-management negotiation simulation. Using real data, one half of the class plays the role of labor union negotiators, and the other half the role of negotiators for corporate management. The two groups of students are given actual numbers from a real case study, different rooms in which to meet, and approximately one hour to prepare. Then the two sides come together to conduct an actual bargaining session on employee benefits. I act as timekeeper, and their goal is to reach consensus on a variety of issues (healthcare, paid vacation, childcare, etc.) by the appointed deadline in order to avert a strike. What the union is unaware of is that management has been given a bottom line figure they may not exceed. Each time I conduct this exercise, class members engage in lively, sometimes heated, debate; adrenalin flows; and rarely is a strike avoided. If I did not choose to conduct this active learning exercise, I might choose to lecture instead on the uses, techniques, costs and benefits of negotiation, and so forth. However, after observing the value of having students "try on behaviors" and work collaboratively in teams, and noticing the "anchoring" that takes place ("Oh, that's what the text means when it remarks about..." "Remember how X, Y, or Z worked when we did our negotiation simulation...?"), I will never return to a standard lecture format on this topic. The abstract becomes concrete, and students ruminate on the experience over the entire semester. They often report in later weeks that they successfully used what they learned during the simulation to buy a car, sell a house, or negotiate a salary. During and after this exercise, students apply, reflect on, and integrate what they have learned actively. However, how I as the instructor frame, describe, qualify, and prepare them for the activity, and how together we process the learning afterwards, makes all the difference. I believe the following suggestions about setting up and debriefing active learning activities can help (Staley, 1999):

Don't make assumptions. One of the most common mistakes instructors make is to assume that students understand why an exercise is being done, what they are supposed to learn, what generalizations can be made, and how the activity applies to other real-world experiences. What seems perfectly obvious to us as teachers is often *not* perfectly obvious to our students.

Set the stage. Demonstrate the activity yourself, particularly at the beginning of a class if it seems threatening or difficult to students. Spend some time making the instructions clear. Uncertainty about how to proceed is disconcerting, and "cleaning up" after pandemonium ensues is much more difficult than giving clear instructions up front. Frame the activity: how does it fit into the course goals, what should students observe during the exercise, why is it included in the first place? Questions such as these up front are important in helping students learn as much as possible during and after the activity.

Announce the time limits and behavioral guidelines. If students know they have 20 minutes to discuss the first set of questions, then they are more likely to pace themselves and finish the set. If they are encouraged to be actively involved but told the noise level must not disturb the class next door, they may be careful to keep their voices at an acceptable level.

Stress the fact that the activity requires a serious attempt to "get real." Role plays, for example, are most instructive when students get a sense of how they might really behave in a similar situation.

Ask students to take part in debriefing. Students can learn from one another's insights during a debriefing session, and this is obviously preferable to simply being told what happened and why. During the debriefing, however, guide their comments. If they begin to criticize an "opponent" or the other team's performance, for example, remind them that the activity was designed to bring out particular behaviors as part of the learning experience, and they should not hold resentment afterwards. In the labor-management negotiation simulation described above, union students sometimes label management as "demanding and stingy" while management students label union members as "greedy and unreasonable."

Organize the activity around people, not just ideas or concepts. Often, as academics, we think in terms of "content, content, content." With first-year students, who are often intimidated and insecure, we should think in terms of relationships, as well (yours and theirs as well as their relationships with one another).

Use active learning experiences as multifaceted learning tools to connect content areas. Chances are any exercise you select will relate to more than one content area of the course, so make certain you gain maximum value from it by "foreshadowing" points that can be revisited as the course progresses.

Simply put, active learning experiences help students bond. One lively exercise will stick with students for a long time, often longer than readings or lectures. Working side-by-side to solve a problem, disclosing information about oneself to a partner—in short, providing opportunities to communicate—lays the groundwork for group intimacy.

Many of the activities in *50 Ways to Leave Your Lectern* will ask your students to apply, reflect, or integrate what they have learned. For example, "Solving the Case" asks students to watch a "visual case study" at the start of class (an extemporaneous skit put on by the instructor and an invited student accomplice) and then *apply* course materials in order to "solve the case." "Five C's Journals" asks students to *reflect* on service learning experiences by writing about "class" (content or readings), "community" (highlights of the service activity), "connections" (intersection points between the two), "contradictions and clarifications" (confirmation, resolution, or continuing questions for further exploration). "Academic Autobiography" requires students to *reflect* on their educational histories, preparation for college, and academic strengths and weaknesses. "The Ideal Student" invites students to create a "Top Ten List" of the characteristics of an ideal college student and then to *integrate* these characteristics into their own behavior.

The exercise called "Diversity Fishbowl" requires extensive processing afterwards. It begins by conducting a discussion with the entire class to identify the kinds of differences that exist between groups of students: male vs. female, left-handed vs. right-handed, tall vs. short, in-state vs. out-of-state, residential vs. commuter, straight-A vs. at-risk, religious vs. non-religious, gay vs. straight, White vs. African-American, etc. Then the instructor chooses one set of features to focus on, and asks the class to divide up accordingly—into left-handed vs. right-handed groups, for example. The minority group forms an inner circle with the majority group surrounding them. The inside group then discusses their experiences *as* a minority group, and the outer circle discusses their experiences *with* the minority group. At this point, no communication takes place between the two groups. The instructor conducts the exercise by beginning with low-threat features and moving to more controversial ones, making choices based on the makeup of the class. After each round, she or he debriefs the two groups together, focusing with sensitivity on the desired outcomes. Based on the comfort level of the instructor and the profile of the class, a range of issues may be explored, from low threat to controversial.

At the end of Part I of *50 Ways to Leave Your Lectern*, you will find an "Active Learning Exercise Evaluation Sheet" to help you decide if exercises here or elsewhere fit your purposes for a particular course. You may find this sheet useful as you design your own activities as well.

Designing Active Learning Experiences

> "During lectures, we deliver the material, but students learn it elsewhere, in our absence. Of course, that happens when we use active teaching and learning strategies, too. Now, however, teachers have daily opportunities to see their students become involved with the course material, with each other, and with them. The excitement of learning is very evident during these interactions. Teachers find themselves smiling a lot as their students discover the subject matter and construct its meaning for themselves. When we work this way with our students we really feel we are teaching, because we witness learning happening directly before us and we know we play a role in catalyzing it. This is enormously satisfying and rather fun, too." (Caprio & Micikas, 1998, p. 218)

If you plan to design your own activity, as opposed to using those contained in *50 Ways to Leave Your Lectern* or another source, here are several things to keep in mind:

1. First, identify both your *general goal* and your specific *ABC goals*. What do you want to focus on? Broadly speaking, what do you want to gain by creating and conducting an active learning exercise? More specifically, what do you want students to feel (*affective goals*), do (*behavioral goals*), and know (*cognitive goals*) as a result of the active learning experience you will design? For example, if your overall goal is to increase students' sensitivity to multiculturalism, what affective, behavioral, and cognitive goals make up the larger goal? Do you want students to develop more positive attitudes toward people of other faiths (affective); visit a church, synagogue, or mosque of another religion and journal about the experience (behavioral); understand, learn, and write a report about the tenets of another religion (cognitive)? What other sorts of activities might accomplish your overall goal of developing cultural sensitivity—eating foreign food, watching a travelogue video, making a native craft, "living" the culture for a week/month/year as an exchange student, etc.?

2. Beyond your general goal, identify specific *learning objectives*. Continuing with the example above, what specific aspects of multiculturalism do you want students to learn? Create an exercise around these specific objectives. If you want students to a) recognize prejudice in others, b) assess their own prejudices, and c) create strategies to reduce prejudice, you might design an activity in which groups with particular identifying features are vying for scarce resources. As competition mounts, the groups may respond more aggressively toward each other. If characteristics of the groups seem strange or unfamiliar, this factor may exaggerate negativity further. An active game (such as "I'm OK; You're…" later in this book), which "brings out the worst" in the competing groups

(without getting out of hand), may make a point that will not be forgotten, that is, increase sensitivity and help students learn specific objectives much more than a lecture or reading on the subject. A template, such as the one used for each of the activities in Part II of *50 Ways to Leave Your Lectern*, is available at the end of Part I to help you design your own activities.

Assessing Active Learning Experiences

> "For many of us, the Learning Paradigm has always lived in our hearts. As teachers, we want above all else for our students to learn and succeed. But the heart's feeling has not lived clearly and powerfully in our heads. Now, as the elements of the Learning Paradigm permeate the air, our heads are beginning to understand what our hearts have known. However, none of us has yet put all the elements of the Learning Paradigm together in a conscious, integrated whole." (Barr & Tagg, 1995, p. 14)

For many teachers, the prospect of including more active learning experiences in their classes raises questions: "How will I grade students' performance? *Can* active learning activities be graded? The text-lecture-test format was easy; now what do I do?"

First of all, it is important to note that many of the activities contained in *50 Ways to Leave Your Lectern* may be used to introduce or reinforce lectures. If a class session is long enough, a lesson plan that moves between a lecturette to set up a topic, discussion to involve students, and interactive exercises to heighten motivation and application—variety in your methods—can be an optimal use of time. Although some activities you use may substitute for a lecture, this book is not about "abandoning" one's lectern forever; instead, it is about expanding our repertoires to require more than one type of sensory and intellectual involvement, which may include listening to a lecture, to reach as many learners as possible. Only you know your own degree of willingness to experiment, your own comfort zone, and your particular students' needs. Including more active learning experiences does not necessarily mean that the exams and quizzes you have used in the past are no longer appropriate. On the other hand, as you expand your teaching methods, you may also need to expand your assessment tools.

The American Association for Higher Education's Assessment Forum (Astin et al., 2001) has outlined nine principles for good practice in assessing student learning:

1. The assessment of learning begins with educational values.

2. Assessment is most effective when it reflects an understanding of learning as multidimensional, integrated, and revealed in performance over time.

3. Assessment works best when the programs it seeks to improve have clear, explicitly stated purposes.

4. Assessment requires attention to outcomes but also and equally to the experiences that lead to those outcomes.

5. Assessment works best when it is ongoing, not episodic.

6. Assessment fosters wider improvement when representatives from across the educational community are involved.

7. Assessment makes a difference when it begins with issues of use and illuminates questions that people really care about.

8. Assessment is most likely to lead to improvement when it is part of a larger set of conditions that promote change.

9. Through assessment, educators meet responsibilities to students and to the public.

This well-constructed list takes into account the many contexts of assessment—from the individual classroom environment to an entire campus culture. Like Chickering and Gamson's "Seven Principles for Good Practice in Undergraduate Education," this list can serve as an important checklist for good practice in assessment.

However, in any discussion of assessment, we must define our terms carefully. The terms *assessment*, *evaluation*, and *grading* share common characteristics, but also have different purposes and applications (Azwell, in Foyle, 1995). Practically speaking, most of the questions raised about assessing active learning actually focus on new ways to evaluate the learning and subsequent grading that occur when we teach in new ways. Assigning grades is easily the least liked aspect of teaching, and in some ways, the *practice* of grading seems in opposition to what we *preach*. Can we go the extra mile to motivate, engage, and support our first-year students—and then fail them? (One could ask: *who* has failed?) Yet, evaluation plays a critical role in the learning process because it gives our students—and us—feedback on how we have done and what we must do better in the future. If active teaching means that we work to motivate, engage, and support our first-year students to help influence their feelings, thoughts, and behaviors, then our evaluation must reflect these priorities. For example, rather than only assess the amount and accuracy of facts and concepts they have memorized, we must assess how they communicate and work with others during the learning process—the *process* in addition to the *product* of learning.

According to Angelo (1991), student learning should be assessed in the four dimensions that coordinate with what and how we teach:

1. Declarative learning (Learning What). This has always been the primary focus of assessment, from kindergarten through graduate school—learning the content of a particular discipline.

2. Procedural Learning (Learning How). What is learned is not enough; students must also learn the skills, processes, and procedures—both general and specific—of a discipline.

3. Conditional Learning (Learning Where and When). Although conditional learning receives less emphasis, it is essential that students learn when and where to apply the knowledge and skills they have mastered.

4. Reflective Learning (Learning Why). To become truly educated lifelong learners, students must reflect on why they feel, think, and act as they do.

In keeping with the philosophy espoused here, allow me to conclude Part I with specific thoughts about assessing active learning experiences:

1. Assessment must be aligned with ABC goals and course objectives. If we clearly define and articulate those goals before creating a learning experience, we can measure progress against them.

2. Share these ABC goals and learning outcomes with your students. Students need to know specifically our goals for them. They, too, are charting a course, and ideally, the destination should be identified before beginning the intellectual journey.

3. In keeping with the spirit of active learning, assessment should be a collaborative process. (See the activity, "What's in an A?" in Part II.) Many instructors have moved to a triangulated grading process in their active learning classes so that student performance is measured in terms of self-evaluation, peer evaluation, and instructor evaluation.

4. If you consider active participation to be critical to active learning, evaluate it. Marchese (2001) reminds us: "you 'gotta be there' to learn the most important parts of any job.... You're not suddenly a physicist because you've memorized the formulas in a textbook; the community of practice called physics consists of expert practitioners who have their own, internal rules and store of tacit knowledge, an unwritten, sixth sense that tells them what constitutes an interesting question, a good experiment, or a viable theory. Book knowledge has a role, but it's only part of the story: The most important learning is always 'situated in practice'." "Wake-Up Call" in Part II can be used at the beginning of a course to demonstrate the importance of participation. If you have concerns that introverts may be less willing to participate in class, allow email dialogue to count as well.

5. Assessment should be focused on future learning as well as past performance. The feedback loop is sometimes ignored, but assessment data must have practical value.

6. Assessment should help faculty continuously improve both process and product: how we teach and what we teach.

7. Assessment should be multifaceted, not only so that we obtain reliable results, but also so that a variety of learning styles is included.

Active learning and today's students: Marchese (1998, p. 4) sums it up well: "Maybe the first step to recovery is to acknowledge that we have indeed a problem of student disengagement. We are part of that problem and our leadership is essential to addressing it. The agenda here is full: to understand before we scapegoat; to make cause with the schools; always to teach imaginatively; and to keep thinking about the ways this society brings young people into valued adult roles. Our goal should be to help students recapture what they knew as third-graders—the deep joy and power of learning."

In the end, the role we play as instructors of beginning students is critical, for as ancient wisdom tells us, "The end depends on the beginning." (Roman poet, Manlius)

ACTIVE LEARNING EXERCISE EVALUATION SHEET

	NOTES	HIGH	MID	LOW

GOAL ORIENTATION
  Affective?
  Behavioral?
  Cognitive?				

TIME USE
  Fits within class time?
  Assign outside of class?				

THREAT POTENTIAL
  Must students disclose?
  Could the activity embarrass?				

ENERGY QUOTIENT **Is the activity fun, exciting, energy producing?**				
INTEREST QUOTIENT **Will students be interested in the results?**				
EMPHASIS **Content, process, or both?**				
PROCESSING POINTS **Lessons, generalizations, relationships to content?**				

Based on "Evaluating Icebreakers" in Eitington, J. E. (1996). *The Winning Trainer*. Houston, TX: Gulf Publishing Company, 9.

ACTIVE LEARNING EXERCISE DESIGN SHEET
Active Learning Exercise on:_____

ABC Goals:

Affective

Behavioral

Cognitive

Group size:

Time required:

Materials:

Physical setting:

Process:

Variation:

Part II

- Introductory Exercises

- First-Year Seminar Exercises

- Content-Integrating Exercises

- Lecture-Based Exercises

- Skills- Based Exercises: Speaking, Writing, Technology

- Discipline-Specific Exercises

- Closing Exercises

Introductory Exercises

One of the most critical aspects of your first-year course is *building* the group, forming one cohesive whole from many separate individuals. Although this is a much greater challenge in a large class than with a smaller group, the exercises in this section are intended to help you:

- **Help students feel comfortable**. For many students, beginning any new venture involves some degree of threat. They may be thinking: How will others react to me? What will I actually gain in this class? What can I contribute?

- **Get students involved**. The best way to reduce anxieties and increase comfort is to get students involved right away. They will be much more willing to listen to you as the teacher if you're willing to listen to them. While this must be done without totally relinquishing control of the class, it's important to do it.

- **Encourage connections among students—and with you**. While cultivating a relationship with your students is important, research tells us that student-student interaction is the most important source of influence on growth and development during students' college careers (Astin, 1993).

✓✓✓✓✓✓✓✓✓✓✓
1, 2, 3, 4, 5... 25
Things We Have in Common
✓✓✓✓✓✓✓✓✓✓✓

Goals: to provide an interesting way for students to get to know one another, discover commonalities, and build class community

Group size: any size class, broken into groups of approximately five students

Time required: any portion of normal class time

Materials: paper and writing utensil

Physical setting: any classroom setting

Process: On the first day of class, ask students to form groups with approximately five members and generate a list of twenty-five things they have in common. Students will generally first identify extremely obvious characteristics (for example, "We are all human beings," "We all have two eyes," "We all go to this school.") and then move to less obvious characteristics that require discussion, for example:

1. We are all taking more than six credits.
2. We all live on campus.
3. We all like _____ (a particular musical group or TV show).
4. We have all seen a movie within the last week.
5. We are all single.
6. We all are eager to start college.
7. We all have pets.
8. We all have tattoos.
9. We all bought the book for this class.
10. We are all Catholic/Protestant, etc.

Encourage students to be creative. You may make the exercise competitive, awarding a prize or recognition to the group that finishes first or simply stop the exercise after 15 minutes, for example, and see which group has the highest number of commonalities.

Variation: Adjust the number of features to your time constraints or the group's sophistication level, or access an incoming group's knowledge of course content as in "Twenty-five Things We Know About Calculus."

Group Résumé

Based on "Group Resume" in Silberman, M. (1995). *101 ways to make training active.* Johannesburg: Pfeiffer & Company, 49-50.

Goals: to help students meet and develop teamwork skills

Group size: any number of participants; however, presentations take about five minutes per group

Time required: 30–45 minutes or more

Materials: One sheet of newsprint and several markers per group; masking tape

Physical setting: Students will need room to spread out and write on tables or on the floor.

Process: Ask students to create a group résumé highlighting the characteristics they bring with them that can help them succeed in college or in a particular major or course. You may wish to create a sample similar to the one below. After groups have completed the task, ask them to hang the newsprint sheets on the walls to create a gallery and/or present their résumés to the rest of the group.

Variation: The résumé may focus more specifically on a particular part of the course such as time management.

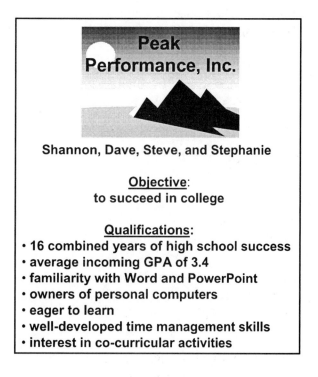

Peak Performance, Inc.

Shannon, Dave, Steve, and Stephanie

Objective:
to succeed in college

Qualifications:
• 16 combined years of high school success
• average incoming GPA of 3.4
• familiarity with Word and PowerPoint
• owners of personal computers
• eager to learn
• well-developed time management skills
• interest in co-curricular activities

These Are a Few of My Favorite Things

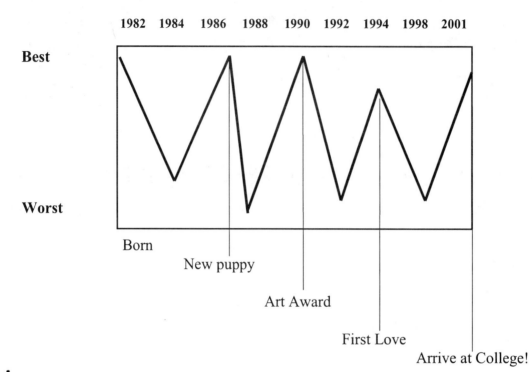

1982 1984 1986 1988 1990 1992 1994 1998 2001

Best

Worst

Born

New puppy

Art Award

First Love

Arrive at College!

Goals: to help students disclose and develop group intimacy

Group size: small groups of 3–5 students

Time required: 30–40 minutes

Materials: One large sheet of newsprint and colored marker for each student

Physical setting: a large room so that students can stretch out on the floor to draw and arrange themselves in groups around the room

Process: Ask students to draw a graph that identifies their favorite memories—the high points of their lives. Tell them that they should identify things they are comfortable disclosing. After they have finished drawing their graphs, ask students to discuss them in small groups. Focus on the high points; asking them to disclose low points is not a good idea since it may cast a depressing tone on the exercise and even require counseling skills to process.

Variation: You may ask students to list particular kinds of events, for example, events relating to schooling.

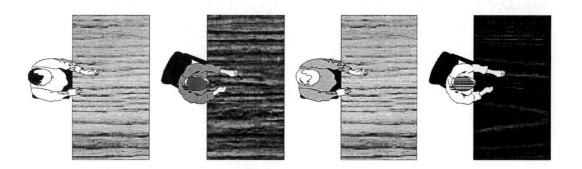

FULL EMPLOYMENT

Goals: to provide an icebreaker conversation topic to each individual student

Group size: any size class

Time required: any portion of normal class time

Materials: a "job description" for each student such as those on the following page (cut into strips)

Physical setting: any classroom setting

Process: On the first day of class, give each student a "job description" for a task to complete during the class session. Many first-year students are reticent at first, and introverts, in particular, will appreciate being given "permission" to meet other students. Students may do their jobs during a break, during a designated introductory period, or even sometime outside of class before the next meeting. Use "Full Employment" to lead to another exercise, such as "Get a Job," or to a general discussion of the "job requirements" of being a college student and what it takes to succeed. You may also have students sign their slips on the back when they have completed their job and use them for another purpose such as a drawing for a PayDay candy bar as "wages," or another upbeat close to the class session.

Variation: Write a list of job descriptions yourself to fit your particular course or the characteristics of the specific students you are working with.

1. Tell someone why you decided to attend this school.

2. Tell someone about your best friend in high school.

3. Ask someone which other classes s/he's taking this term.

4. Ask someone a question about the course textbook.

5. Give two other students a sincere compliment.

6. Ask to look at someone else's notes.

7. Tell someone something you've heard about this course.

8. Share something you've learned so far in one of your classes.

9. Shake hands with someone before you leave class today.

10. Tell someone what you like best about your hometown.

11. Share a story about one of your favorite teachers.

12. Ask someone what time it is.

13. Ask someone about the weekend weather forecast.

14. Ask someone what s/he thinks of college so far.

15. Ask someone where s/he's living.

16. Ask someone to borrow a pen.

17. Tell someone what you're most looking forward to in college.

18. Smile at every student in the class.

19. Tell someone you've appreciated his/her comments during class.

20. Ask your instructor for clarification on a point s/he made.

If You Could Read My Mind

Goals: to help students introduce themselves to one another in a lively, low-threat activity

Group size: any size class

Time required: 30–45 minutes

Materials: self and partner Mindreader's Sheets (on following pages) for each participant

Physical setting: any setting in which individuals can get together in pairs, but *make sure participants are seated next to someone they don't know*

Process: Ask students to form pairs and fill out the two Mindreader's Sheets, one with their own responses and another speculating on how their partner would respond. The "d" option is "fill-in-the-blank" for instances in which "a," "b," and "c" are not descriptive and a better alternative can be written in. After individuals have filled in the blanks, each member of the dyad then takes turns "reading the other's mind." *They must base their projections on nonverbal cues before any dialogue takes place between them.* Participants may discuss the accuracy of their responses after each item or after they have speculated on all the items on their partner's list, and they should talk about the cues they used to make their projections.

Variation: Additional questions may be created; however, statements should not be threatening or require participants to disclose personal information early in a course. After working in pairs, you may elect to have two pairs, or foursomes, work together reading each other's minds or discussing the exercise. The value of the exercise is that it gives students a "buddy" on whom to rely when they know no one in the group.

MINDREADER'S SHEET
Self

1. If I won a million dollars, the first thing I'd buy would be
    a. a new condo   b. a new car   c. a trip abroad   d. _____

2. Most people probably don't realize I
    a. am very shy   b. am very sensitive   c. am very nervous   d. _____

3. The most important quality in a friend is
    a. loyalty   b. trustworthiness   c. a sense of humor   d. _____

4. I consider myself to be a(n) _____ person.
    a. happy   b. motivated   c. interesting   d. _____

5. I prefer to be
    a. by myself   b. with one friend   c. in a group   d. _____

6. I wish I were more
    a. confident   b. optimistic   c. assertive   d. _____

7. My favorite form of relaxation is
    a. sports   b. movies/TV   c. books   d. _____

8. What I am most attracted to in another person is
    a. looks   b. brains   c. personality   d. _____

9. What I want most from others is
    a. affection   b. admiration   c. respect   d. _____

10. Many of the world's problems could be solved if there were more
    a. love   b. trust   c. kindness   d. _____

MINDREADER'S SHEET
Partner

1. If my partner won a million dollars, the first thing s/he'd buy would be
   a. a new condo   b. a new car   c. a trip abroad   d. _____

2. Most people probably don't realize my partner
   a. is very shy   b. is very sensitive   c. is very nervous   d. _____

3. My partner believes the most important quality in a friend is
   a. loyalty   b. trustworthiness   c. a sense of humor   d. _____

4. My partner considers him/herself to be a(n) _____ person.
   a. happy   b. motivated   c. interesting   d. _____

5. My partner prefers to be
   a. by him/herself   b. with one friend   c. in a group   d. _____

6. My partner wishes s/he were more
   a. confident   b. optimistic   c. assertive   d. _____

7. My partner's favorite form of relaxation is
   a. sports   b. movies/TV   c. books   d. _____

9. What my partner is most attracted to in another person is
   a. looks   b. brains   c. personality   d. _____

9. What my partner needs most from others is
   a. affection   b. admiration   c. respect   d. _____

10. My partner thinks many of the world's problems could be solved if there were more
    a. love   b. trust   c. kindness   d. _____

GRAFFITI STATIONS

GOALS: to help students share fears, needs, and expectations about the class

GROUP SIZE: 10–50 students

TIME REQUIRED: 30 minutes to 1 hour

MATERIALS: flip-chart paper, markers, masking tape

PHYSICAL SETTING: walls that will accept masking tape, wall space to create a gallery around the room

PROCESS: Ask students to circulate around the room and finish statements such as the following written at the top of sheets of newsprint you have taped to the walls:
"If only teachers would …"
"My hopes (fears) about taking this course include …"
"If only students would …"
"I'm ideally suited to major in _____ because …"
"If there's one thing I could change about myself as a first-year student, it would be …"
After everyone has signed each sheet or during a break, students may circulate and read others' comments.

VARIATIONS: This exercise may be used to explore students' reactions to controversial issues, current events, topics of general interest, or issues that relate to their new roles as new first-year students. Instead of stem sentences, you may ask students to respond to controversial images printed from websites (KKK, Hitler, etc.); however, be advised that processing the exercise may be challenging if negativity emerges.

Harry
Potter
Fan

Party
Animal

Country
Music
Lover

Ski
Buff

Sports
Enthusiast

On with your Hat!

Goals: to help students introduce themselves to the class in a creative, low-threat, enjoyable way

Group Size: any size class; although, if the group is too large, the exercise may have to be conducted in small groups

Time required: any portion of normal class time

Materials: as many hats as you can find around the house or buy inexpensively from a second hand or novelty store: baseball cap, straw sun hat, visor, stocking cap, veil, scarf, chef's hat, cowboy hat, etc. Be creative!

Physical Setting: any classroom setting; a circle works well

Process: Ask students to select a hat from those on display that characterizes them in some way, and use the hat as a prop to introduce themselves to the class. After putting on a hat and explaining why they chose it, they may go on to describe their high schools, their families, their intended major, jobs they've held, why they chose your college, etc. Today's students seem to enjoy wearing hats, and this exercise can be fun and produce interesting results. Students may select a hat another student has previously used; however, encourage them to choose a different hat that communicates another important aspect of themselves or give a different reason for choosing the same hat.

Variation: Have students bring unusual hats to introduce themselves, and put all the hats on display for anyone to choose from.

Post Office

Goals: to help students get to know one another and get answers to their questions about the course or the campus

Group size: any size class

Time required: any normal class session (or time outside of class)

Materials: an index card for each student

Physical setting: any classroom setting

Process: On the first day of class, give students an index card. On one side, they should write their names, and on the other, a question about your class, about the textbook, about another course, or about the campus, for example. Collect the cards and redistribute them, making sure that students don't get their own cards back. The challenge of the exercise is twofold: 1) to find the author of the new question they've received and provide him or her with an answer (even if the answer is "Gosh, I don't know!") and 2) to be found by the student holding their original card, get an answer, and get the card back. Students may complete the exercise by milling around during class or break, or outside of class before the next meeting.

Variation: Suggest that students' questions focus specifically on the reading assignment or other course content.

Based on "Wanted Posters" in Pike, B, & Busse, C. (1995). *101 games for trainers*. Minneapolis: Lakewood Books, 87.

Goals: to provide a low-threat, interesting, and enjoyable way for students to introduce themselves to one another

Group size: any size class

Time required: any portion of normal class time and additional time outside of class, if desired

Materials: a "RAP Sheet" for each student such as the one on the following page, scotch tape or stapler or glue to adhere photos, and a Polaroid camera

Physical setting: any classroom setting

Process: On the first day of class, take a snapshot of each student with a Polaroid camera. Hand out the "RAP Sheets" and ask each student to fill in the blanks describing him or herself and then attach the photo. (If you want to make the exercise more challenging, take profile "mug shots," instead of head-on, full-face snapshots.) Students may then introduce themselves, one at a time, by reading and talking about their descriptions. At the end of class, redistribute the RAP Sheets so that each student receives one describing someone else, and ask each student to "Recognize and Pursue" his or her partner outside of class, somewhere on campus or in another class, and return the sheet to him or her before the next meeting. After discussing the results during the following class session, you may allow students to keep their RAP Sheets as "souvenirs" of their first day of college (an interesting reminder years later) or post them on your office door, all at once or feature one student per week, for example.

Variation: If students commute from home and have access to family photos, you might consider asking them to bring baby or childhood photos. This adds an interesting twist, since students must guess who's who based on current appearance.

PHOTO

"RAP" (Recognize And Pursue) Sheet

Alias_____

Born on _____

Originated in _____

Distinguishing features include _____

Best known for_____

Often seen with_____

Last attended (school)_____

Often seen wearing_____

Works at_____

Has a pet ___ named _____

Can often be found_____

Sometimes consumes large quantities of_____

Most positive qualities are_____

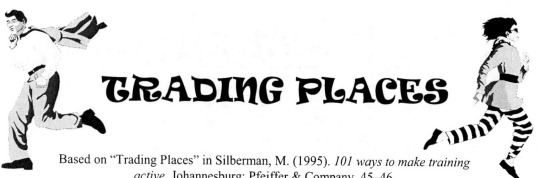

TRADING PLACES

Based on "Trading Places" in Silberman, M. (1995). *101 ways to make training active.* Johannesburg: Pfeiffer & Company, 45–46.

Goals: to help students get acquainted and identify their positive qualities

Group size: relatively unlimited

Time required: 10–20 minutes

Materials: a pad of sticky notes (one note per participant)

Physical setting: a large room so participants can circulate

Process: Ask students to identify a positive quality, characteristic, or experience that would set them apart from others in the group. They should list a descriptive word or phrase on a sticky note and stick it to the front of their shirts. Next ask them to circulate around the room, reading one another's notes, "hawking" their unique attributes, and trading with others whose qualities, characteristics, or experiences they would like to have. At the conclusion of the exercise, engage students in a discussion of why they chose their particular attributes and why they traded for other ones.

Variation: Students can give themselves other identities (famous people, etc.) from current events or from history.

What's in a Name?

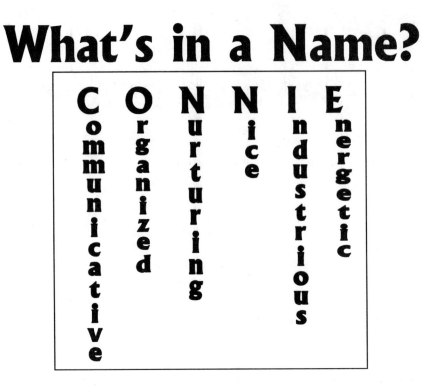

Based on "Name Cards" in Eitington, J. E. (1996). *The winning trainer.* Houston, TX: Gulf Publishing Company, 7.

Goals: to provide a creative way for students to get to know one another

Group size: any size class

Time required: any portion of normal class time

Materials: paper and writing utensil

Physical setting: any classroom setting

Process: As an introductory exercise on the first day of class, ask students to create a name diagram such as the example above by listing the letters of their first names across a sheet of newsprint or other large sheet of paper and finding adjectives to describe themselves that begin with those letters. The degree of challenge inherent in the exercise will vary depending on the student's names (Zachary vs. Bob). After students complete their diagrams, they should disclose the results in small groups, followed by introductions in the larger group, if time permits. (Students with challenging first names may then first solicit suggestions from their small group members.)

Variation: Early in the term but after students know one another, ask them to complete the exercise using one another's names and traits they have observed.

Wheel in a Wheel

Based on "Circle-to-Circle Ice Breaker" in Pfeiffer, J. W. (1989). *The encyclopedia of group activities: 50 practical designs for successful facilitating.* San Diego: University Associates, 97–99.

Goals: to help students introduce themselves to one another during a lively activity

Group size: 20–40 participants (instructors, student mentors, freshmen)

Time required: 15–30 minutes

Materials: One chair per participant

Physical setting: Form two concentric circles with the same number of chairs facing each other (one inside the other) in a large room. If an odd number of participants exists, the extra person may read the statements below to the group. Chairs are preferable to sitting on the floor since participants will move from spot to spot to change partners. Standing in a large area indoors or outdoors works very well, too.

Process: Ask students to select a seat facing another participant in one of the two concentric circles. Read the first statement below and ask participants to respond to their "partners." After both partners have responded to the statement, at your command or at the blow of a whistle, for example, students sitting in the outer circle should move clockwise one seat. Students in the inner circle should remain stationary. When everyone is reseated, proceed to the next statement, etc.

"I believe in…"
"Most people don't think much about…"
"One of my pet peeves is …"
"An important quality I look for in people is…"
"What I like most about our school is…"
"My biggest hope about this course is…"
"If there's one thing I could change about myself as a college student, it would be…"
"If I had time to spare, I'd…"
"I'm happiest when I…"
"If only other students would…"

Variation: Additional statements may be created; however, statements should not be threatening or require students to disclose personal information early in a course.

THE LINEUP

GOALS: to energize, get acquainted, build group cohesion, and lead into other exercises

GROUP SIZE: any size class

TIME REQUIRED: approximately 30 minutes

MATERIALS: list of features

PHYSICAL SETTING: large classroom or outside

PROCESS: First identify high and low poles on opposite walls of the room. Then ask students to line up on an imaginary line in between, according to gradations of features such as height, birth date, alphabetical order of first or last names, length of time they've lived in the state, number of siblings, etc. Each ordering should be a timed event, with the group continually trying to reduce its previous time. After exploring simple features, move to academic information that eventually leads to a discussion of college or course success factors: number of students in their largest class, number of textbooks they bought, hours they plan to study per week, etc. Following this exercise, move to another exercise such as "Get a Job," "Spending Time," or a general discussion of what it takes to succeed in college or in a particular course.

VARIATION: If the group is too large, this exercise may be done in smaller groups of six, for example, as a competition.

You ARE What You Read!

Finding the Love of Your Life

Chicken Soup for the Sports Fan's Soul

1001 Reasons to Think Positive

Goals: to provide a creative way for students to get to know one another

Group size: any size class

Time required: any portion of normal class time

Materials: copies of "YAWYR" sheets (a sample follows), preferably ones you create yourself, and a writing utensil

Physical setting: any classroom setting

Process: You can create your own "YAWYR" sheets easily by toggling back and forth between a website such as amazon.com and PowerPoint. Choose book images from the website that you think would best represent the interests of your particular student population and paste them onto a PowerPoint page. As an introductory exercise on the first day of class, ask students to fill out a "YAWYR" sheet individually and then to use it as a tool to introduce themselves to one another in pairs, in a small group format, or to the entire group. The exercise serves the purpose of beginning the course with a subtle but creative emphasis on reading, which is often *not* the leisure-time activity of choice among today's students.

Variation: If you work with nontraditional students, you may wish to choose books with subject matter that relates directly to the workforce, childcare, time management, or other issues they face.

You ARE What You Read!

Although you may not have read these specific books, each represents an area of endeavor many people value in their lives. Of the 12 books pictured below, identify those that best represent your values, and list the reasons for your choice beside each book.

The 22 Non-Negotiable Laws of Wellness By Greg Anderson		**Chicken Soup for the Sports Fan's Soul** by Jack Canfield (Ed.)
Looking Good by Nancy Nix-Rice and Pati Palmer		**1001 Reasons to Think Positive** by Ella Patterson
Conditioning for Outdoor Fitness By David Musnick et al.		**Finding the Love of Your Life** by Neil Clark Warren, Denise Silvestro (Editor)
The New York Times Guide to the Best 1000 Movies Ever Made by Vincent Canby et al.		**The Inner Game of Music** by Barry Green, W. Timothy Gallwey
Why Religion Matters: The Fate of the Human Spirit in an Age of Disbelief by Huston Smith		**The Courage to Give** by Jackie Waldman, Janis Leibs Dworkis, Joan Lunden
The Complete Directory to Prime Time Network and Cable TV Shows by Tim Brooks, Earle Marsh		**Relationships in Progress** by Pamela B. Brewer, Lisa Wilkinson (Editor), Sandy Weber

HOLLYWOOD
(OR WHATEVER CITY YOU LIVE IN)
SQUARES

Based on Montgomery, R. J., Moody, P. G., & Sherfield, R. M. (1997). *Cornerstone: Building on your best course manual.* Boston: Allyn & Bacon (contained in a handout received at the 17th Annual National Conference on the Freshman Year Experience, Columbia, South Carolina).

GOALS: to help students become acquainted in an interactive setting

TIME REQUIRED: 15–20 minutes or longer, depending on the size of the group

MATERIALS: handout on the next page and a piece of scrap paper for each student

PHYSICAL SETTING: normal classroom

PROCESS: Ask each student to write down one thing on a piece of scrap paper that no one in the group could possibly know about them (but that they wouldn't mind sharing). For example:

a) "I had oatmeal for breakfast this morning."
b) "My mother was born in Pittsburgh."
c) "The living room of my house is painted pink."

After students hand in their sheets of paper (without their names), read each statement aloud and ask participants to write a key word from each statement, one per block, on the handout (in any order). After all blocks are filled with key words, ask the group to circulate and quickly fill in the names that belong with each statement. They should ask other participants, "What did you have for breakfast this morning?" instead of "Which statement did you write?" Ask students not to give themselves away.

VARIATION: You may play this game at the end of the term to reinforce course content: "What will you remember most about this course?"

_____ **SQUARES**

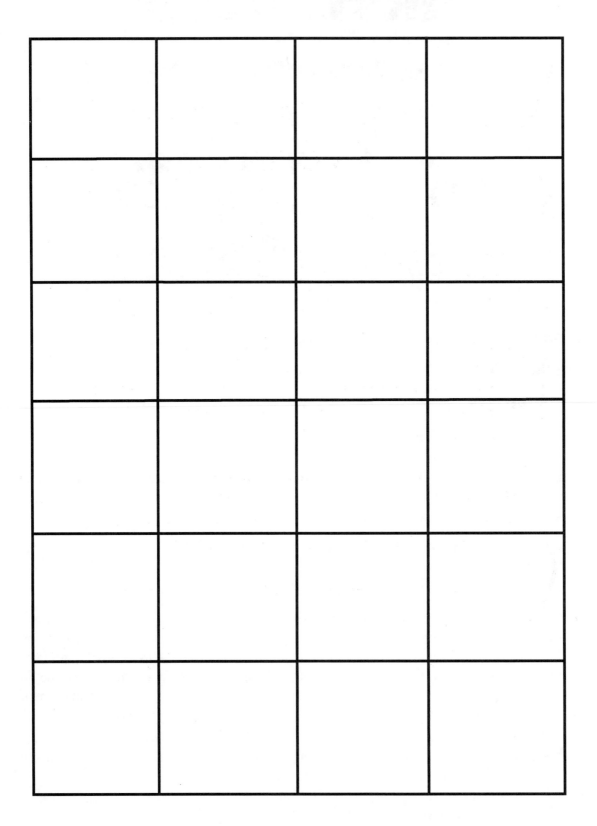

First-Year Seminar Exercises

Research indicates that students participate more and experience less fear in First-Year Seminars, as opposed to most discipline-based classes, and they are more satisfied with their amount of participation (Reynolds & Nunn, 1998). The exercises in this section are intended to help students:

- **Understand and begin to build the array of cognitive, affective, and behavioral skills that are critical to college success.**

- **Preview the value of a First-Year Seminar course.**

- **Begin the process of value clarification that typically takes place during the first year of college.**

- **Evaluate their strengths, weaknesses, and readiness as learners.**

SPENDING TIME

GOALS: to help students understand the costs of education and the consequences of not managing their time through a memorable, hands-on demonstration

GROUP SIZE: any size class

TIME REQUIRED: 20–30 minutes

MATERIALS: a large stack of one-dollar bills and information on your institution's costs

PHYSICAL SETTING: normal classroom

PROCESS: Ask students to help you calculate the hourly cost of attending college at your institution. For example, begin by listing the cost of room and board for one semester (and dividing by X number of weeks, 7 days/week, 24 hours/day, etc.); books; health insurance; tuition; clothes; spending money; student fees; transportation; computer; supplies; entertainment; and so on. After all the calculations are done, ask a student to count out the number of dollar bills that equal the average hourly cost. Note other desirable items that could be purchased for that amount, and communicate that choosing to cut class is the equivalent to throwing money ($ times hours) away. Make the point that academic success depends on *spending time* wisely.

VARIATION: You may wish to vary this exercise by bringing stacks of pennies, nickels, and dimes, and asking participants to stack currency based on how they allot their time, with pennies representing low-priority items, nickels representing medium-priority items, and dimes representing high-priority items. Ask them to compare their current priorities with those that lead to college success and create an action plan to change their behavior.

Ad Team Members: Julie, Jason, Amy, and Jeff

TURN ON
to University Seminar!

University Seminar:
· motivates you to learn
· raises your GPA
· increases your technology skills
· refines your speaking and writing
· introduces you to campus resources
· develops time management skills
· get you involved in co-curricular activities

Group Ad

Goals: to help students realize the value of a First-Year Seminar course and build teamwork skills

Group size: any number of students, divided into small groups

Time required: 30-45 minutes, depending on the size of the group, or done outside of class as a homework assignment

Materials: one sheet of newsprint and marker per group; masking tape

Physical setting: Students will need room to spread out and write on tables or on the floor.

Process: Ask students to create an advertisement selling the benefits of the First-Year Seminar. You may wish to create a sample similar to the one above. After groups have completed the task, ask them to hang the newsprint sheets on the walls to create a gallery and/or present their ads to the rest of the class.

Variation: The ad may focus more specifically on a particular part of the course such as time management. The activity may also be expanded by allowing students to use a variety of advertising media: television (PowerPoint), newspaper (write an ad or column about the course for the school paper), product creation with "jingle" (re-label a bottle of "Dr. Pepper" with the professor's name, "Dr. _____"), etc. This activity works particularly well at the end of the course (before course evaluations!) to help students realize the many gains they have made in their First-Year Seminar class.

Academic Autobiography

Based on a contribution from Frank Bell, Iowa State University,
Wadsworth workshop, St. Louis, March 2000.

Goals: to help first-year students think about how prepared they are for college

Group Size: any size group

Time Required: completed by students outside of class as a paper or journal assignment

Materials: none

Physical Setting: home or residence hall

Process: Challenge your students to reflect on their academic backgrounds:

"At some point in your schooling, you've probably written an autobiography about your life. In this assignment, you'll be writing about your *academic* life. How well have you been prepared through grade school, middle school, and high school for the scholarly requirements of college? What are your strong points as a student? What do you predict will be your biggest academic challenge in college? This assignment asks you to focus on yourself as a student, both by looking back and by looking ahead."

Variation: Allow students to read each other's academic autobiographies by posting them on the class website or bring them to class to compare their experiences.

CULTIVATING CLASSROOM CIVILITY

GOALS: to help first-year students understand acceptable and unacceptable behaviors in college classes

GROUP SIZE: any size

TIME REQUIRED: approximately 30 minutes to 1 hour

MATERIALS: necessary props (for example: baseball cap, cell phone, cigarette, food, bubble gum, soft drink, an accomplice to help you stage demonstrations, etc.)

PHYSICAL SETTING: normal classroom or lecture hall

PROCESS: This exercise is an excellent way to help students understand that particular behaviors that were acceptable, tolerated, or even perceived to be "cool" in high school are not acceptable in college classrooms.

1. Demonstrate with negative role modeling.

Based on past experience and the type of civility issues your institution faces, decide which unacceptable behaviors you would like to demonstrate. At the beginning of the term, demonstrate these behaviors yourself: come to class wearing a baseball cap backwards (with your business suit) and begin class normally; prearrange to have someone call you on your cell phone, take the call and chat; have someone come to the door and summon you for a conversation, stay by the door and confer; take a mouthful of food and continue talking; leave and come back with a soft drink; chew bubble gum (and blow bubbles); stop and put your head down on the desk for a short nap, etc.

2. Clarify specific positive and negative behaviors.

Often, we assume first-year students have been prepared for the college classroom during high school; however, this is not always the case. Whether the behavioral issue is committing plagiarism, engaging in side conversations, or violating your school's computer ethics rules, students often arrive at college with misperceptions or few perceptions at all about acceptable behavior. We cannot expect students to know and understand our expectations unless we clarify them.

3. Write expectations into the syllabus.

Describe your expectations both verbally and in writing by including specifics in a section on classroom decorum in your syllabus.

4. Use learning contracts.

The exercise named "The Ideal Student" is an excellent way to clarify "behavioral" issues; it can also be used as a template for contracts related to *learning*, as opposed to *behavioral*, goals.

5. Generate classroom rules together.

One way to generate buy-in is to work with students to generate classroom rules together. Based on their high school experiences, first-year students may have important ideas to contribute, and a collaborative approach can serve as a bonding experience for the group. When rules are generated together, students are also more willing to monitor each other's behavior, and peer critique can be an important motivator.

VARIATION: Other props can be used for negative role modeling; be creative!

First-Year Seminar
Course Scorecard

Goals: to help students become more responsible for their own success and track their progress in the course

Group size: relatively unlimited

Time required: 10–20 minutes to explain the concept; progress noted throughout the course

Materials: One scorecard (on following page) per student which details the requirements for the course (assignments, attendance, participation, etc.)

Physical setting: Students keep scorecards in their possession for the term (instructors may keep copies for their own record keeping as well) and hand them in at the end of the term.

Process: A First-Year Seminar helps students develop motivation, responsibility, and accountability. Using a scorecard can make these responsibilities become visible and tangible and help students realize that other courses require similar upkeep. Tailor the scorecard to display the course requirements. Copy the scorecard onto brightly colored, heavy cardstock. Ask participants to keep track of their progress and point accumulation throughout the duration of the program/course and to try to achieve as many points as possible.

Variation: Tailor the scorecard so that it includes your school/program logo or other relevant information.

First-Year Seminar

Name _____

COURSE SCORECARD

	Discussion	Attendance	Quizzes						TOTAL
Possible									
My score									
Possible									
My score									

The Royal Runaround

Goals: to provide a creative way for students to learn their way around campus

Group size: any size class

Time required: any portion of normal class time or as an out-of-class assignment

Materials: the questionnaire that follows and a writing utensil

Physical setting: any classroom setting

Process: Give students the attached questionnaire and send them off, either during class or as homework, to find the listed items.

Variation: Expand on the items listed on the questionnaire or write new ones based on your particular campus.

The Royal Runaround

1. The Office of the Dean of _____ is in (bldg)_____, (room)_____.

2. The best-kept-secret place to eat on or near campus is _____.

3. The best place to park on or near campus is _____.

4. The best place to live on or near campus is _____.

5. The most attractive piece of art on campus is located _____.

6. The largest classroom on campus is _____.

7. The easiest access to a computer on campus is _____.

8. The reference librarian on duty right now is _____.

9. The full names of three people who are *not* in this class are _____,
   _____, and _____(get signatures).

10. The best place to meet people on campus is _____.

11. A popular professor on this campus is _____ (get signature).

12. The best place to get medical attention on campus is located _____.

13. The best place to buy books and class materials is located _____.

14. The best place to get tutoring or counseling if you need help is _____.

15. The Admission/Registrar's office is located in (bldg)_____, (room)_____.

16. The best place around to buy an ice cream cone is _____.

17. The place to pay your college bill in person is located _____.

18. List one fact you didn't already know from the campus website _____
    _____.

19. Who is the head of the Psychology Department?_____.

20. The phone number for the English Department is _____.

The Ideal Student

Goals: to identify behavioral standards and to help students accept responsibility for their own performance in a course

Group Size: normal class/group size

Time Required: generally 45 minutes to 1 hour, but dependent on the size of the group to some extent

Materials: newsprint and easel stand, black/white board, or blank transparency and marker

Physical Setting: normal classroom

Process: Ask students to think about the characteristics of an ideal student and, as a homework assignment, to create their own "Top Ten List" to bring to the next class session. In class, ask students to read and explain their own lists of the characteristics of an ideal student. Begin to synthesize individual lists by creating a class "master list" (on the board, a flip chart, or blank transparency) on which all students can agree. Then ask students to write down items 1–10 on the class list and identify the items they will promise to do during the course by initialing each line, writing a "Y" for "yes," or making some similar marking. Suggest that they consider their decisions carefully since the results will be collected and reviewed by you throughout the term. Use these lists to monitor the performance of individual students, make midcourse corrections, and help students work toward improvement.

Variation: At midterm, redistribute the lists so that students are reminded of the "contracts" to which they agreed and rediscuss the class list.

Diversity Fishbowl

Based on "The Fishbowl" in Pike, B. & Busse, C. (1995). *101 games for trainers*. Minneapolis: Lakewood Books, 28.

Goals: to help students reflect on the differences between majority and minority groups and lead to a better understanding of relevant issues

Group size: any size class although a smaller class works best; a large group would require using representative volunteers instead of the entire group

Time required: whatever portion of normal class time you decide to set aside

Materials: none

Physical setting: a classroom large enough to form two concentric circles of chairs (or students may sit, kneel, etc. on the floor)

Process: Begin a discussion with the group to identify the kinds of differences that exist between groups of students: male vs. female, left-handed vs. right-handed, tall vs. short, thin vs. heavy, in-state vs. out-of-state, residential vs. commuter, straight-A vs. at-risk, religious vs. non-religious, gay vs. straight, White vs. African-American, etc. Choose one set of features to focus on, and ask the class to divide up accordingly—into left-handed vs. right-handed groups, for example. Ask the minority group to form an inner circle with the majority group surrounding them. The inside group should discuss their experiences *as* a minority group, and the outer circle should discuss their experiences *with* the minority group. At this point, no communication should take place between the two groups. Conduct the exercise by beginning with low-threat features and moving to more controversial ones, making choices based on the makeup of the class. After each round, debrief the two groups together, focusing with sensitivity on the outcomes you desire from the exercise.

Variation: Vary the features based on "hot" issues on your particular campus. If you select highly controversial features, you may ask students to role–play being members of either group, as opposed to identifying their own actual membership.

I'm OK; You're...?

Based on "Culture Mates: A Cross-Cultural Simulation" in Silberman, M. (1996). *The 1996 McGraw-Hill Training and Performance Sourcebook*. New York: McGraw-Hill, 5–9.

Goals: to help students recognize cultural differences and assess their own values

Group size: 20–50 students

Time required: 30 minutes to 1 hour

Materials: "Subcultural" descriptions (see following page), one subculture for each student

Physical setting: a room large enough for students to circulate

Process: Give each individual a paragraph description of his/her subculture's values and behavior. (Individuals should *not* see one another's descriptions.) Their task is to find at least one other individual in the group who belongs to the same subculture. They should do this by following the "rules" printed in their paragraphs, but they may not simply ask others which subgroup they belong to. They should make a mental note of which other students may be members of their subgroup. Stop the exercise after 5–10 minutes, and discuss the questions below.

1. How did you feel about your subculture? Why?
2. How did you feel about other subcultures? Why?
3. How does this experience relate to new freshmen?
4. What do you find challenging about interacting with individuals from another culture?
5. What can we learn from having done this exercise?

Variation: Additional subcultures may be created based on particular content or process goals. It may also be useful to have groups create their own subculture descriptions after you explain the purpose of the exercise.

SUBCULTURE A

This is a very *friendly* subculture. Smiling is the normal facial expression people display. When greeting others, you should laugh, blink three times, and look them straight in the eye. This culture has no spoken language.

SUBCULTURE B

This is a very *shy* subculture. Eye contact is avoided at all costs. Looking at another person is considered to be obscene. You should not initiate interaction. You may speak to others, but you must do so without ever looking at them.

SUBCULTURE C

This is a very *grouchy* subculture. In this subculture, people scowl at one another. You may communicate with others, but you should give the impression that communicating is a total waste of time.

SUBCULTURE D

This is a very *outgoing* subculture. People talk continuously about anything and everything. You should greet others by saying "Hey, hey, hey, whad'ya say?" and shaking hands with your left hand.

SUBCULTURE E

This is a very *noncommunicative* subculture. Individuals are uncomfortable communicating and they enjoy solitude. You should not be rude to others, but you should let them know you'd rather not interact.

What's the Difference?

Based on "Defining Diversity" in Pike, B. & Busse, C. (1995). *101 games for trainers.*
Minneapolis: Lakewood Books, 11.

Goals: to help students reflect on the many ways in which individuals differ and the fact that each of us is unique

Group size: any size class

Time required: approximately 30 minutes

Materials: a set of Crayola "Multicultural" crayons (with eight different skin tones, available from www.crayola.com on-line for approximately $3 per set) for a prize

Physical setting: a normal classroom setting

Process: Ask students to form pairs and begin listing all the various ways in which they differ: age, height, gender, eye color, hometown, etc. Tell them a prize will be awarded to the pair with the longest list at the end of five minutes. The point of the exercise is to begin a discussion on the meaning of diversity, to note that diversity is more than skin color, and to recognize that each individual is unique. Stop the pairs after five minutes, find out which pair won, ask them to read their list, and award the prize. Other pairs may add features they discovered. This exercise works well to introduce and define diversity.

Variation: Try the exercise with groups rather than pairs of students.

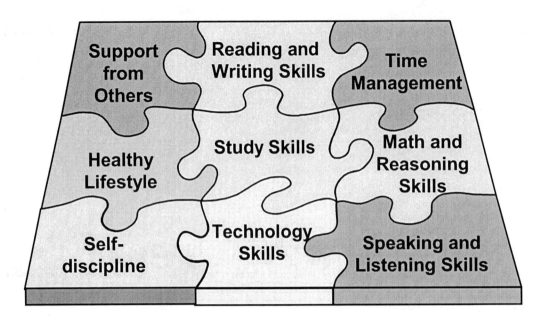

Success Puzzles

Goals: to help students identify the most important components of college success by working collaboratively and exchanging thoughts with other students

Group size: any size class

Time required: approximately 30–40 minutes

Materials: template (one template per nine students, or any number if you make your own template)

Physical setting: any classroom setting

Process: After a preliminary headcount of your class, reproduce the template that follows as many times as necessary on cardstock and cut each template into pieces. (You should have as many puzzle pieces as students in your class.) You may use the exercise as an icebreaker by distributing the individual pieces, one per student, and asking them to find partners who have pieces that correctly complete their puzzle. (You may ask students to form groups with others holding pieces in the same color if you wish.) After the groups are assembled, ask students to work together to label each piece of the puzzle with an important component of college success. What factors must a student possess in order to be successful in college? Many factors may be proposed, but ultimately, the group must agree on the most important factors to complete their "Success Puzzle." The group should have clear reasons for selecting these final choices and eliminating others that were originally proposed. After all groups have finished the task, each group should share its "Success Puzzle" and the class as a whole can compare puzzles and discuss results of the exercise.

Variation: Have student groups create their own puzzles and swap with another group or buy blank puzzle sets (available at some stationers as party invitations).

An Integrated Education at Work in the Real World

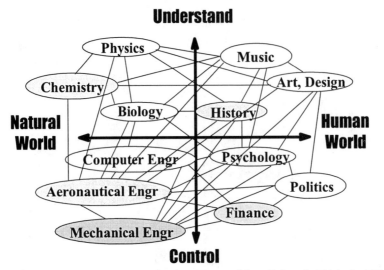

Guest author: Dr. Steve Staley, Professor of Humanities, Colorado Technical University

Goals: to demonstrate the interconnectedness of knowledge. Often first-year students—or students at any level—think of courses (and disciplines) as boxes to check off as they complete their education.

Group Size: any size group, even up to a full lecture hall

Time required: 20–35 minutes

Materials: slides or transparencies such as those below

Physical setting: any, but students must be able to communicate in small groups

Process (background):

A Framework for a Unified, Integrated, Useful Education

Two simple questions about education:　　　(Fig. 1)

1. WHAT do we study?

2. WHY do we study?

WHAT DO WE STUDY AND WHY? (Fig. 1): Begin by asking students two fundamental questions about the university: "What do we study?" and "Why do we study?" You'll get all sorts of specific answers (English, Math). But if you push for an overall answer, sooner or later someone will yell out "Stuff" or "Everything."

Capitalize on this answer—yes, we study "everything" (uni-verse). But a convenient and meaningful way of putting it is to say that we look at everything in two opposite directions. We look outward, into the *natural* world; and we look inward, into the *human* world (Fig. 2).

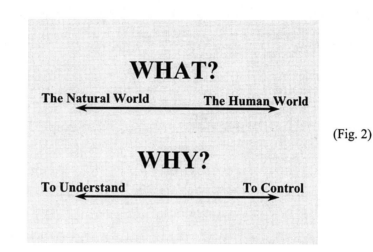

(Fig. 2)

At the most idealistic and theoretical end of the scale, we study *to understand* things. We're naturally a curious species, and we want to know how gravity works, why is there air, why is the sky blue, why are parents so hard to reason with, how does the Congress work (or maybe why it sometimes doesn't). But at the most practical end of the scale, we study not just to understand things, but also *to control* them—to make things and people do what we want them to do. We want to "control" concrete and steel to make better bridges, "control" the flow of information through computers, make taller buildings, better social programs, more powerful weapons, more expressive art, more insightful novels—maybe even better, stronger, faster, healthier, smarter people. (Note: The word "control" is the correct scientific term to use here; it does not mean *manipulate* in a pejorative or Machiavellian sense, but rather *do something with, use,* or *change* as opposed to merely *understand* intellectually.)

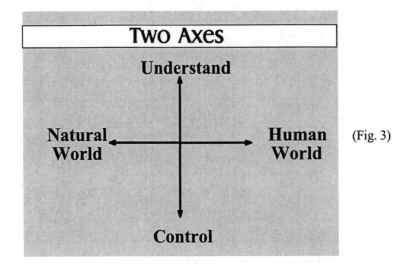

TWO AXES (Fig. 3): Rene Descartes, the seventeenth-century French mathematician and philosopher, taught that if you really want to understand how two things interact, put them on perpendicular axes. When you do that, look what happens.

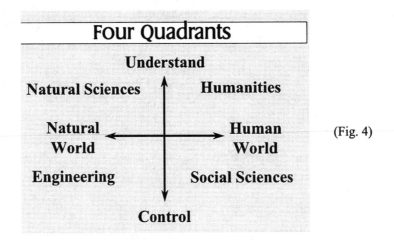

FOUR QUADRANTS (Fig. 4): What do we call the university departments that try to *understand*

- the natural world? The **Natural Sciences** (physics, chemistry, biology, etc.)
- the human world? The **Humanities** (history, literature, philosophy, etc.)

And what do we call the disciplines that help us to *control*

- the natural world? The **Engineering Sciences** (mechanical, electrical, computer, etc.)
- the human world? The **Social Sciences** (political science, economics, sociology, etc.)

What we see in the matrix now is a direct reflection of the university. In fact, many universities are divided into Colleges or Divisions or Area Requirements similar to these.

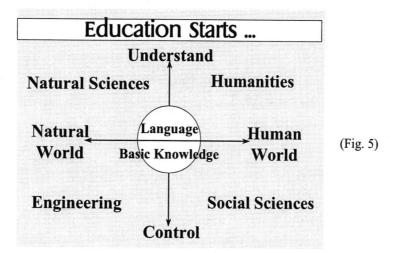

(Fig. 5)

THE PROCESS OF A COLLEGE EDUCATION—LANGUAGE AND BASIC KNOWLEDGE (Fig 5): When does one's education start? At birth, really—it starts right in at the center of the matrix and blows up like a balloon through grade school and high school, with language and basic knowledge:

- Language—information transfer and manipulation
  - Natural languages—English, Spanish (listen, speak, read, write)
  - Artificial languages—math (counting, operating), even computer languages
- Knowledge—common knowledge of our society (basic stories, behavior, ethics, science, history)

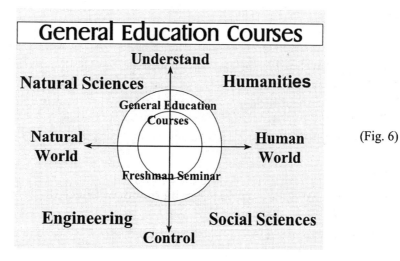

(Fig. 6)

GENERAL EDUCATION COURSES (Fig. 6): Your university may require "general education" or "core" courses. Ask your students to give examples of the courses they'll be taking in their first year at the university. At some institutions, Freshman Seminar is the core of General Education.

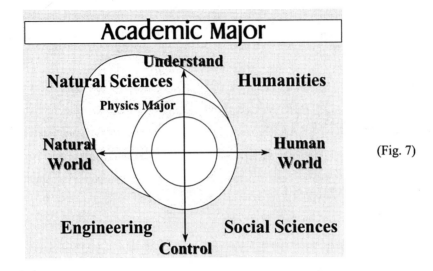

(Fig. 7)

ACADEMIC MAJOR (Fig. 7): On top of these basic broadening courses, students will also take many courses in their academic majors—say, in physics. So a student's map will continue to grow outward, but with a bulge in the direction of a major. It's skewed, but it still includes all four regions.

An Integrated Education at Work in the Real World (exercise):
Ask students to work in groups of two or three. They should imagine they've graduated from the university a few years ago, and are now rising young managers with a large American corporation—in this case, say it's Boeing. The boss calls one morning to tell them she's naming them to a planning team which will do the preliminary brainstorming work on the next-generation jumbo jet—the Boeing 797—which will be marketed worldwide in competition with European, Asian, Russian, and other American aircraft. Their team is to come up with a concept for the new plane which will win that competition as the best overall design in the world. What various academic disciplines will their team have to draw upon as it develops its plans? Surely aeronautical engineering—that's obvious. But what other knowledge and skills will members have to bring to the table?

After several minutes, have the groups begin listing their suggestions. If you are using a blank overhead, write them down in the appropriate quadrant, demonstrating visually the integrated nature of a truly productive education at work in the real world.

Variation: You may devise a similar application project, other than a hypothetical 797 jet, for students to collaborate on.

Journal Coupons

Goals: to emphasize time management and sound decision making

Group size: any size class

Time required: little or no class time

Materials: coupons reproduced from the graphic above or created using pre-perforated ticket forms available from office supply stores.

Physical setting: a normal classroom setting

Process: Early in the term, when you are discussing accepting responsibility for one's own learning (perhaps immediately before or after you have done "The Ideal Student" exercise), give each student two coupons. Tell the students that each of their college courses will require behind-the-scenes preparation, even if the syllabus lists "midterm" and "final exam" as the only two requirements for a grade. Talk about reading, taking notes, studying, highlighting, etc. as the kinds of behind-the-scenes preparation for which they will be responsible. Announce that at various points during the semester, students feel overwhelmed with many assignments due at the same time. The coupons will release them from two journal assignments during the term; however, only two coupons may be used. Extra coupons may not be redeemed, so it will be necessary to plan ahead. If only a few journals are required, distribute only one coupon. Coupons must be submitted in advance, as opposed to *after* a journal was due. They are intended to be used as a time management tool.

Variation: Try using the ticket idea for other creative purposes, such as an out-of-class social event.

VALUES FOR COLLEGE, CAREER, and LIFE

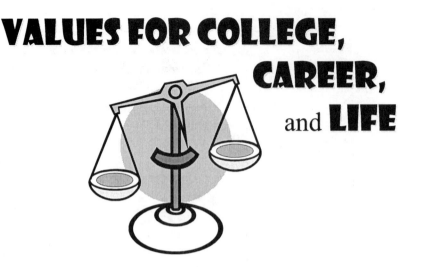

GOALS: to provide an interesting way for students to begin to examine their existing values, to compare their values to those of their classmates, and to reflect on, reinforce, or change them as a result

GROUP SIZE: any size class, broken into groups of approximately five students

TIME REQUIRED: any portion of normal class time

MATERIALS: one or more of the Values Ranking Sheets that follow and a writing utensil

PHYSICAL SETTING: any classroom setting

PROCESS: Ask students to fill out one or more of the Values Ranking Sheets (with their highest priority item as #1) individually and then to compare them in groups with approximately five members. After discussing their individual rankings, group members should collaborate to create a group ranking with which everyone can agree. The final column on the Value Ranking Sheet asks students to identify reasons why their original rankings differed from the final group rankings. After the groups have finished, they may send a representative to the board to post their rankings. Each group should be prepared to defend its decisions.

VARIATION: Another way to conduct the exercise is to ask students to cross out their least important item, one round at a time as you announce it, to see which value is left remaining as their single most important. (The first value deleted should be labeled #9 for last place, and so forth, in order to keep track.) In this case, simply white out the column headings on the master sheets and have students write in new ones such as "Rationale."

COLLEGE VALUES

	My Ranking	My Group's Ranking	Explanation of Difference
Finding a life partner			
Getting top grades			
Getting into grad/prof school			
Having a busy social life			
Finding profs to mentor			
Preparing for a career			
Becoming a lifelong learner			
Graduating with honors			
Achieving an important goal			

77

CAREER VALUES

	My Ranking	My Group's Ranking	Explanation of Difference
Satisfying work			
Good colleagues			
Travel opportunities			
Comfortable income			
Chance to be my own boss			
Good benefits			
Attractive surroundings			
Chance to be creative			
Sense of achievement			

LIFE VALUES

	My Ranking	My Group's Ranking	Explanation of Difference
Satisfying career			
Happy family life			
Desirable life partner			
Comfortable income			
Good health			
Attractive appearance			
Opportunity for fame			
Strong friendships			
Sense of achievement			

Follow the Lecturer

| AM. HISTORY 100 | PHYSICS 101 | INTRO TO BUSINESS | AFRICAN-AMERICAN STUDIES |
| Professor Lincoln | Professor Einstein | Professor Iococca | Professor Parks |

Goals: to help students recognize instructors' lecturing styles and improve their listening and note-taking skills

Group Size: any size group

Time Required: dependent on the size of the group

Materials: a "Lecture Style Analysis" worksheet for each student

Physical Setting: normal classroom

Process: First-year students, who are more likely to be visual or interactive learners than auditory ones, may benefit from becoming aware of and analyzing how their individual instructors lecture. Some instructors follow the text closely in their lectures, some follow a topical outline, and some jump from one content area to another with seemingly little to link them, especially from a student's perspective. If students pay attention to instructors' lecture styles, then they can adjust the way they listen and take better notes. Ask students to help you create a worksheet they can bring to each of their classes (inconspicuously, of course, so that they don't make their instructors self-conscious), and use their analyses to help them do their best in each of their courses.

Variation: Create a worksheet yourself, like the one on the following page, and distribute it to save class time.

LECTURE STYLE ANALYSIS WORKSHEET

COURSES:

EMPHASIS Content, students, or both?				
ORGANIZATION Structured or spontaneous?				
PACE Fast, slow, or medium?				
VISUAL AIDS Used? Useful?				
EXAMPLES Used? Useful?				
LANGUAGE Terms defined? Vocabulary understandable?				
DELIVERY Animated via body language?				
QUESTIONS Encouraged?				

GET A JOB

Goals: to help students understand that being a college student has real requirements and responsibilities just like a "real" job in the world of work

Group size: 15–40 students

Time required: 45 minutes to 1 hour

Materials: large sheets of newsprint and examples of employment ads from a local newspaper

Physical setting: normal class/training room

Process: Ask participants or small groups to create classified employment ads for the "job" of college student. For example, "_____ College/University is seeking applicants with excellent skills in oral and written communication, problem solving, time management, and technology for positions as professional students preparing for a variety of future opportunities.... " Ads should list particular job requirements, benefits, information about your institution, and so on, and be transferred to a large sheet of newsprint to present to the larger group.

Variation: You may wish to have each participant first create an ad individually, perhaps as an outside assignment, and then combine and refine their ideas in groups.

So Much to Do—So Little Time:
A Student In-Basket Exercise

GOALS: to help students learn to prioritize and sequence activities

GROUP SIZE: any size class

TIME REQUIRED: approximately 30 minutes

MATERIALS: a "So Much to Do—So Little Time" sheet for each student

PHYSICAL SETTING: any classroom setting

PROCESS: An in-basket exercise is a management simulation that provides practice in decision making. Typically, it is composed of 15 or 20 items, all of which must be analyzed and acted upon relatively quickly. Participants are told to assume they are new to a management position, for example, and that they must first begin by investigating the in-basket of their predecessor to see if particular items need immediate attention. This activity for students is similar in that they are presented with a fairly long "to do" list and asked to rate and rank the activities based on criteria they themselves generate. After students complete the exercise individually, get them together as a group to discuss their ratings, rankings and criteria. You may wish to use this activity to introduce a unit on time management and to discuss time management criteria, such as a "mapping" approach (what you can do on the way to doing something else), a "grouping" approach (activities that require a phone or car; activities that are on-campus or off-campus, etc.), or point out the differences that sometimes exist between what is "urgent" and what is "important."

VARIATION: Instead of using the "So Much to Do—So Little Time" sheet that follows, create a list of your own sheet that includes real campus activities and course requirements.

So Much to Do—So Little Time

Start time: 9:00 a.m., Monday morning, Pacific Daylight Time,
during the second week of the Fall semester

Assume that all the activities below must be done today (Monday). In each blank, give the item a priority rating between 1 and 3, with 1 indicating "top priority" and 3 indicating "this can wait." Finally, cross out the item numbers and renumber them to indicate which you would do first, which second, and so forth. On the back of this sheet, list the criteria you used to make your decisions.

1. _____ Return Professor Jordan's call before class tomorrow. He left a message saying he wants to talk to you about some problems with your LIT 101 paper.

2. _____ Pick up your paycheck at McDonalds and get to the bank before it closes at 5:00 p.m. this afternoon.

3. _____ Call the new love interest in your life and ask about going to the party together this weekend before someone else does.

4. _____ Visit the Speech Center to get critiqued on your first speech due Friday. It's closed evenings.

5. _____ Call your aunt. She lives on the East Coast (EST). Today is her 40th birthday.

6. _____ Stop by the Health Center to take advantage of free flu shots today only.

7. _____ Listen to the new CD you bought yesterday.

8. _____ Leave a note, asking your roommate to please stop monopolizing the phone. It's really aggravating.

9. _____ Read the two chapters in your History textbook for the in-class quiz on Wednesday.

10. _____ Watch the first episode of the new "Reality TV" show you've been waiting for at 9 p.m. tonight.

11. _____ Write a rough draft of the essay due in your composition class on Thursday.

12. _____ Check with your RA about inviting an old high school friend to spend the weekend.

13. _____ Return the three rented videos that are a week overdue.

14. _____ Call your math TA and leave a message asking for an appointment during her office hours to get help with the homework due on Wednesday. Nearly everyone is confused about the assignment.

15. _____ Go to the campus Athletic Banquet tonight at 6 p.m. to receive your award.

84

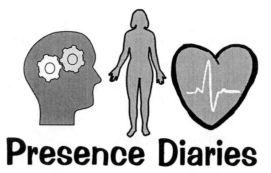

Presence Diaries

Based on Jacob, S. W., & Eleser, C. B. (1997). Learner responsibility through "presence."
College Student Journal, 31, 460–66.

Goals: to help first-year students become more aware of their mental, physical, and emotional states; detect obstacles to attentiveness; and assume responsibility for their own learning by being "present."

Group size: any size class

Time required: approximately 5–10 minutes at the start of class

Materials: one index card per student for each class session

Physical setting: any classroom setting

Process: Many students, but particularly first-year students, are often unaware of their own obstacles to learning. When they first enter the classroom, they may not be conscious of their intellectual, physical, and emotional states, or realize how these states either facilitate or interfere with learning. At the beginning of class, ask students to answer the following three questions on note cards:

1. Describe your *mental* state: Are you ready to learn? (i.e., Do you know today's topic? Have you completed the reading? Did you bring assignments to turn in?)
2. Describe your *physical* state: What do you sense? (i.e, Do you have a headache? Are you hungry, tired, energized?)
3. Describe your *emotional* state: How are you feeling? (i.e., Are you stressed, anxious, motivated, elated?)

This exercise is based on a semester-long "Responsibility Through Presence" project in which freshmen and seniors rated themselves on these (and other) characteristics at the beginning of each class, wrote a brief narrative in their journals describing their "presence" in class on that day, and periodically graphed their scores. Overall results indicated that freshmen rated themselves lowest in "physical" presence and highest in "mental" presence. For example, 86 percent of freshmen complained of physical distractions: colds, lack of sleep, sore throats, etc.; 81 percent of freshmen described emotional concerns: financial worries, deaths or sickness in their families, personal relationships, etc. At the end of the term, 88 percent of freshmen reported that the presence-rating project had helped them become more aware of factors that affected their learning.

Content-Integrating Exercises

The activities in this section are intended to help students:

- Become engaged in course content.

- Integrate course components in ways that are meaningful to students.

- Gain competence and confidence by teaching other students.

- Reflect on and react to what is happening during class or in assigned readings.

PROJECT-BASED LEARNING: AN INTRODUCTION TO RESEARCH PERSPECTIVES

This activity forms the course structure for the Transition Seminar for transfer students at the University of Colorado at Colorado Springs; team taught by the author with Kathryn Andrus (Art History) and Daryl Prigmore (Physics).

GOALS: to help students begin to understand the nature of research and the comparative research perspectives of the humanities, social sciences, and natural sciences

GROUP SIZE: any size class, but optimally a number divisible by three and no more than thirty students total

TIME REQUIRED: an extended project over several weeks

MATERIALS: research topics and perspectives (such as those on the following template), cut into strips

PHYSICAL SETTING: any classroom setting (and time outside of class)

PROCESS: Project-based learning works well with students at any level, including first-year students. At the start of this activity (which could be employed after "An Integrated Education at Work in the Real World"), each student draws a slip of paper identifying a research PERSPECTIVE and a research TOPIC. Research perspectives include the following: 1) arts/humanities or AA (Aesthetic Aspects), 2) social sciences or PP (Public Perceptions), and 3) natural sciences/engineering or TT (Technical Tradeoffs). Make sure each perspective is reproduced on a different pastel color: AA list on pink, PP list on blue, TT list on yellow, for example. Research topics could include anything that works for your purposes. In this example, the focus is on the city/town/area in which your institution is located—particularly helpful for out-of-state students who are new to your region. (But even local students will learn a great deal.) Research topics might include economic development, energy, transportation, your campus itself, etc. After students have drawn a slip identifying their topic and perspective, allow them to mingle and find their two research partners who will work on the same topic. After discussing the project and then completing their own research, each threesome (AA, PP, and TT on a single topic) should work together to create a presentation for the class (using PowerPoint, for example). The activity must be supported by introductory readings or presentations distinguishing the three research perspectives (kinds of research questions posed and sources of information), and on-line newspaper archives or library copies of local newspapers may be used to gather information about your area. AA students may also visit museums or search records and archives to find information; PP students may conduct brief surveys or interviews; TT students may consult technical references on-line or in the library. The activity can be a dynamic learning experience!

1. crime   AA

2. energy   AA

3. neighborhoods   AA

4. tourism   AA

5. the university   AA

6. city center   AA

7. transportation   AA

8. economic development   AA

9. media   AA

10. nonprofit organizations   AA

1. crime   PP

2. energy   PP

3. neighborhoods   PP

4. tourism   PP

5. the university   PP

6. city center   PP

7. transportation   PP

8. economic development   PP

9. media   PP

10. nonprofit organizations   PP

1. crime   TT

2. energy   TT

3. neighborhoods   TT

4. tourism   TT

5. the university   TT

6. city center   TT

7. transportation   TT

8. economic development   TT

9. media   TT

10. nonprofit organizations   TT

Reflecting on Service: Five C's Journals

Goals: to help students reflect on service learning experiences

Group size: any size class

Time required: done as an outside writing assignment

Materials: none

Physical setting: any classroom setting

Process: The learning in service learning takes place via effective reflection activities that 1) link experience to learning objectives; 2) are guided; 3) occur regularly; and 4) allow feedback, assessment, and values clarification (Hatcher & Bringle, 1997). Eyler, Giles, and Schmiede (1996) assert that reflection must be continuous, connected, challenging, and contextualized. After or during a service learning experience, ask your students to write triple-entry "Connections Journals" in which they divide their papers (or email attachments) into three sections and a summary section as follows:

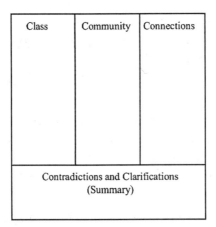

Class	Community	Connections
Contradictions and Clarifications (Summary)		

Students should fill in each section: "Class" (particular points from the course content or readings), "Community" (particular highlights from the service activity), "Connections" (intersection points between the two), and finally a summary section, "Contradictions and Clarifications" (confirmation, resolution, or continuing questions for further exploration).

Case Study Exchange

Goals: to help students learn problem-solving skills and apply course material

Group size: normal class size

Time required: homework assignment; individuals or collaborative groups may analyze in approximately 30–40 minutes

Materials: a case study (narrative/story) written by each student

Physical setting: homework assignment; normal class/training room

Process: Ask each student to write a brief case study or story about a fictitious freshman based on his or her own experiences or those of a friend (using a false name). The case study should focus on a common problem that freshmen experience or a situation that was poorly handled. After papers are turned in, randomly exchange case studies so that each student has a partner. Participants should use course materials and/or a chapter from the text to help the fictitious student described in the case study "fix" the problem or develop strategies that could have been used to prevent the problem from occurring. After the analysis/problem-solving papers are written and graded, return the papers and announce the members of each secret partnership, allowing the pairs time to discuss the analyses they've written.

Variation: Rather than asking each student to write a case study, collaborative groups may write them. Or choose the best individual case studies and distribute one to each group.

Based on "What? So What? Now What?" in Silberman, M. (1995). *101 ways to make training active.* Johannesburg: Pfeiffer & Company, 207–208.

GOALS: to help students summarize, reflect, and plan for the future

GROUP SIZE: any number of students

TIME REQUIRED: will vary by individual; can be done quickly at the close of a session

MATERIALS: e-mail capability, index cards, or paper

PHYSICAL SETTING: a computer lab, in front of a home computer, or during class

PROCESS: Students are asked to answer three questions pertaining to a class meeting: "**What?**" (What transpired? What impressed me? What particular point do I remember?), "**So What?**" (What impact did it have on me, the class, the overall course)? and "**Now What?**" (What will I do about it? How will I change? What are my long-term strategies for the future?) The questions can serve as a framework for weekly journals from freshmen, either on e-mail or as on-paper assignments. (Note: Caution participants to spend the least amount of effort answering the "What?" question since you were there too and know what happened. Sometimes freshmen focus most of their attention on this question because it is "safe" and requires little imagination or risk.)

VARIATION: The formula may be used in many settings as a comprehension check or quick feedback mechanism.

Goals: to motivate students to read the text, learn course material, and work collaboratively

Group size: any size class

Time required: approximately 30 minutes

Materials: a crossword puzzle you create, using terms from the text, generated at http://puzzlemaker.school.discovery.com/CrissCrossSetupForm.html

Physical setting: a normal classroom

Process: Generate a puzzle using course content at the above website. You may allow students to work on the solutions in pairs or small groups, perhaps as a timed competition, or assign the puzzle as homework.

Variation: Ask students to submit their first names along with a brief description on the first day of class, such as "Connie: a redhead from Colorado Springs." Use these names and "definitions" to generate a puzzle for the following session to help students learn one another's names. Or consider having students design puzzles themselves, perhaps with pairs or small groups to whom you have assigned individual chapters.

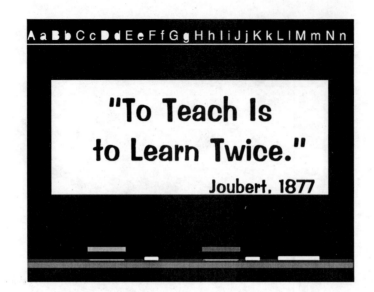

AaBbCcDdEeFfGgHhIiJjKkLlMmNn

"To Teach Is to Learn Twice."

Joubert, 1877

Based on "Jigsaw Learning" in Silberman, M. (1995).
101 ways to make training active. Johannesburg: Pfeiffer & Company, 171–173.

Goals: to help students understand the value of collaborative learning

Group size: ideally, sixteen students, although the exercise can work with a larger number, formed into four-person groups

Time required: 40 minutes to 1 hour

Materials: four sets of handouts on material to be mastered, with each set copied on a different color of paper, and playing cards with four from each suit

Physical setting: room large enough for students to rotate among groups

Process: Initially, divide students into groups by distributing the playing cards. Have all the spades congregate in one location, all the diamonds in another, and so on. Give individuals in each group a handout covering one-quarter of a portion of material to be covered, or one heading out of four, relating to a topic in the course. Each individual's job is to teach his/her content to the other three members of each group s/he rotates to. After approximately 10 minutes, students should rotate to the next group. Tell them they may "teach" using any style they deem to be appropriate. The goal is content mastery. For example, if the topic to be mastered is "Guidelines for Research on the Internet," then introductory materials on the following subtopics could be developed for students to teach one another: Person A—Navigating the Web; Person B—Using Search Engines; Person C—Assessing Information; and Person D—Copyright Issues and the Web. After students have rotated to all four groups, conduct a discussion on the values of collaborative learning, that is, how teaching others helps students learn.

Variation: The exercise can be modified if more students are involved, or another method can be used to divide individuals into groups; for example, you could distribute equal numbers of four types of candy pieces from a bag of Hershey's miniatures, such as Mr. Goodbar, Crackle, milk chocolate, and dark chocolate.

JOURNALS

Goals: to help first-year students relate in-class lectures and activities to their own experiences and keep up with ongoing reading assignments

Group Size: any size group

Time Required: completed by students and responded to by instructors outside of class

Materials: computer access; email program

Physical Setting: home, residence hall, or office

Process: Explain to students that a journal will be due each week by a particular deadline (for example, by Monday at midnight for a Wednesday class, giving you as instructor a day to respond). You may accept actual email journals, or you may require students to send a word-processed attachment. (Since emails are typically informal, requiring an attachment is more likely to produce higher quality writing.) In their journals, ask students to include two parts:

> **Part 1. REVIEW.** Discuss **last week's** in-class lecture, class discussion, or activity in terms of what impressed you most. Write about how this information relates to you personally.

> **Part 2. PREVIEW.** Preview **next week's** reading assignment as listed on the syllabus. What did you find most or least interesting? How did the reading relate to what typically happens in class or in your other courses? What does the reading mean to you?

Variation: Allow students to read each other's R/P journals, particularly at first when they are learning how to complete this type of assignment.

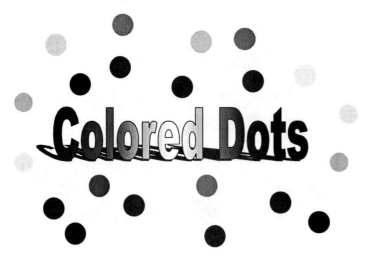

Colored Dots

Based on "Colored Dots" in Solem, L. & Pike, B. (1997). *50 creative training closers*. San Francisco: Jossey-Bass, 21—22.

Goals: to help students focus on course content, assess their level of comprehension, and identify material for further study

Group size: any size class

Time required: any portion of normal class time

Materials: packages of adhesive dots in multiple fluorescent colors, cut in strips

Physical setting: any classroom setting

Process: Often students find that their notes make sense during class while they're being taken, but later they have difficulty determining what various emphasis marks mean (asterisks, arrows, underlining, or scribbled comments). To help students focus on important material, pass out strips of colored dots, which can be purchased in packages inexpensively from an office supply store, for them to use during an exam review session or regular lecture. When they get to a portion they need to study further outside of class or a concept they would like to explore later, they can stick a colored dot beside the item to mark it. Colored dots stand out and make important content areas easier to recognize later. Students enjoy this practice and appreciate the instructor's efforts to ensure their success in mastering course material.

Variation: Colored dots can also be used to mark sections of the text that need to be reread. Their adhesive backing allows them to be removed easily without damaging the paper.

Lecture-Based Exercises

This section is intended to help you lecture with better results by:

- **Pausing to allow students to compare notes and talk through concepts.** Rowe (1980) and Ruhl, Hughes, and Schloss (1987) suggest that pausing to allow pairs or small groups to compare and rework their notes improves retention of information. Menges (1988) suggests that giving a quiz immediately following a lecture may double both factual and conceptual recall after considerable time has elapsed (8 weeks).

- **Helping students apply or use lecture information for problem solving.**

- **Giving students a preassigned task as motivation for listening to the lecture.**

- **Bringing accountability for lecture material into plain view.**

- **Helping students react personally to lecture content.**

COMMUNICATION

Based on *Managerial Psychology,* H. J. Leavitt, University of Chicago Press, 1958, 118–128.

Goals: to demonstrate the challenges of learning via the lecture mode

Group size: any size group

Time required: 30–45 minutes

Materials: Figures 1 and 2 (following)

Physical setting: normal classroom

Process: Ask for a volunteer to describe the two Figures to the rest of the group so that students can replicate them on paper of their own.

Round 1: Ask the volunteer to turn his/her back to the group (to eliminate nonverbal cues) and give the class instructions for drawing Figure 1. No questions from the group should be allowed (one-way communication). Note the exact amount of time taken to give the instructions.

Round 2: Ask the volunteer to face the group and give instructions for drawing Figure 2. Students may ask the communicator to clarify and elaborate as much as is necessary to get the drawing right (two-way communication). Note the exact amount of time taken.

After both rounds of the exercise, ask the group the following questions and fill in the chart that follows:
    --Who thinks their drawing closely resembles the original?
    --What was your reaction during each round?
Ask the volunteer communicator to describe his/her reaction during both rounds.

Finally, show Figures 1 and 2, one at a time, to the group and ask how many students actually did accurately replicate the two Figures. After all cells of the chart are filled in, discuss the implications for learning from lectures.

ONE-WAY VS. TWO-WAY

COMMUNICATION

	Time to complete	Number who *think* they're correct	Number who are *actually* correct	Group reactions	Volunteer communicator reactions
One-way communication (Figure 1)					
Two-way communication (Figure 2)					

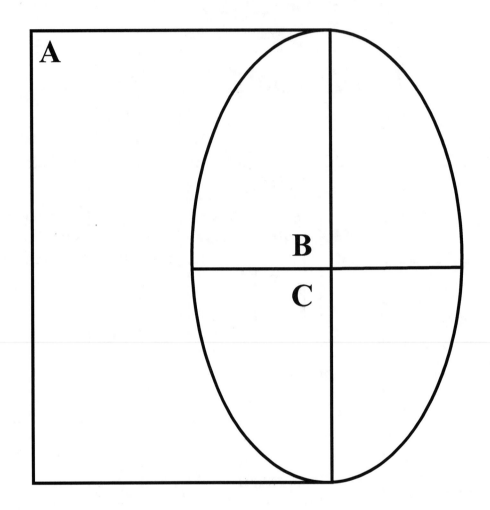

Figure 1

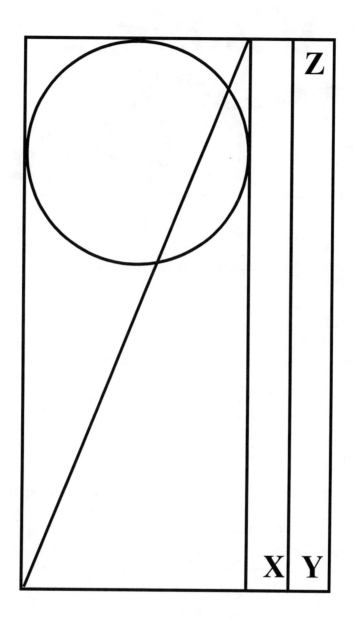

Figure 2

Goals: to make lectures more engaging and help students increase their listening and comprehension skills

Group size: any number of students, even a large lecture class

Time required: continued use throughout the semester, as desired

Materials: a set of colored cards (masters follow, cut pages in half) for each individual; sample questions on overheads or PowerPoint slides

Physical setting: normal classroom

Process: Reproduce each quiz card on different brightly colored cardstock (all "a" letters on red, "b" on blue, and so forth). Give a lecture, or create questions from previously covered material. Stop the lecture at various points and flash a key question on the screen using PowerPoint or an overhead, and on cue, ask participants to hold up the card they think represents the correct answer. The technique gives participants immediate feedback on their listening and comprehension skills (and keeps them on their toes!) and helps instructors gauge how effectively they are delivering course content.

Variation: Visible Quizzes may be used periodically throughout a lecture or at the end, for exam review, or immediately after a written quiz to verify and discuss correct answers one at a time, either individually or collaboratively in groups.

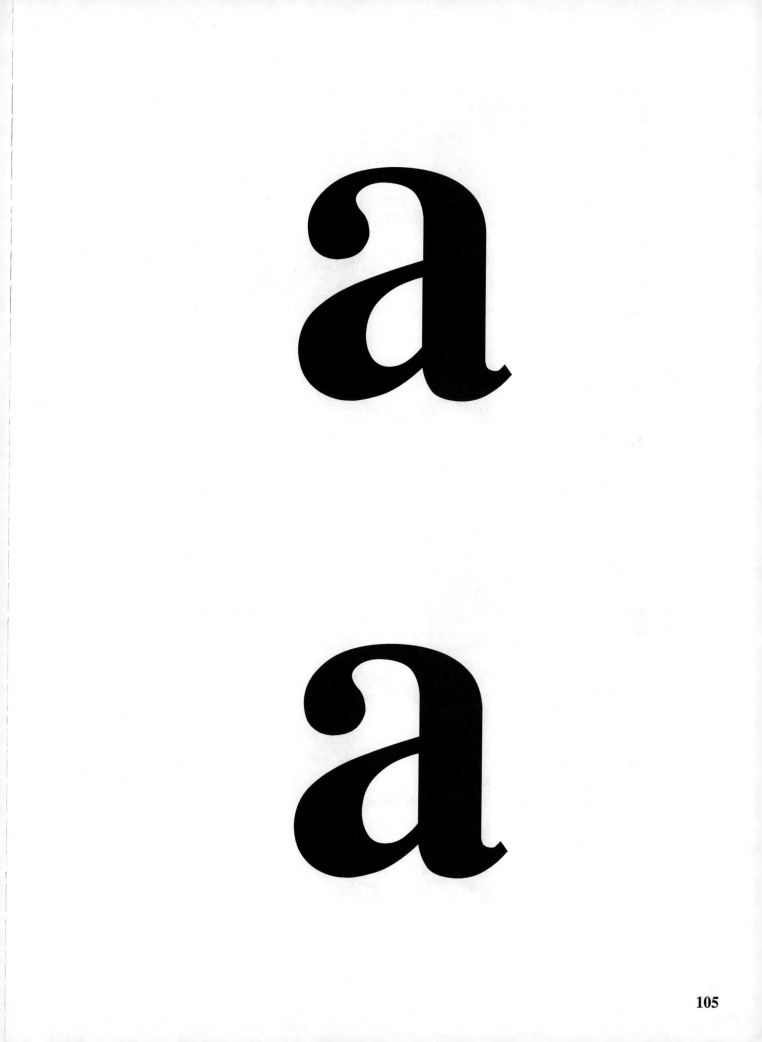

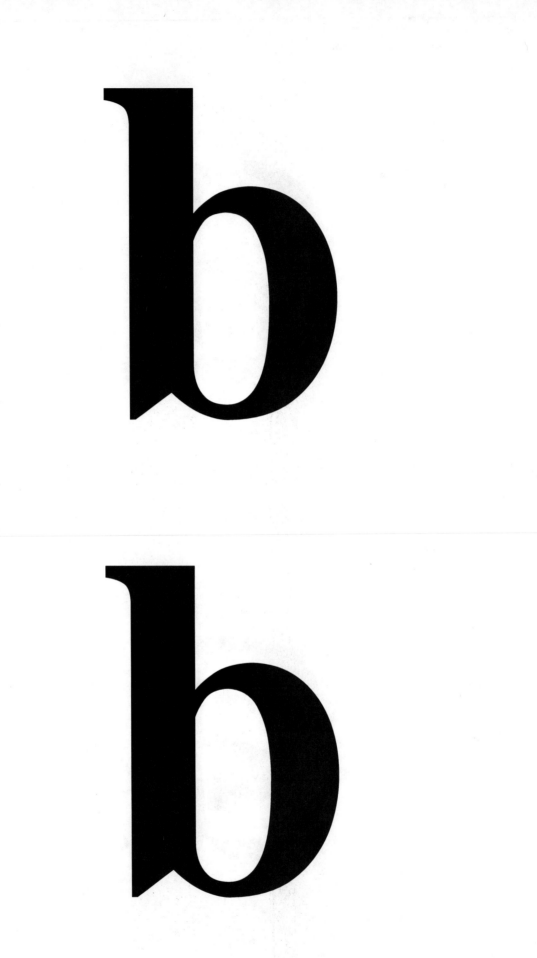

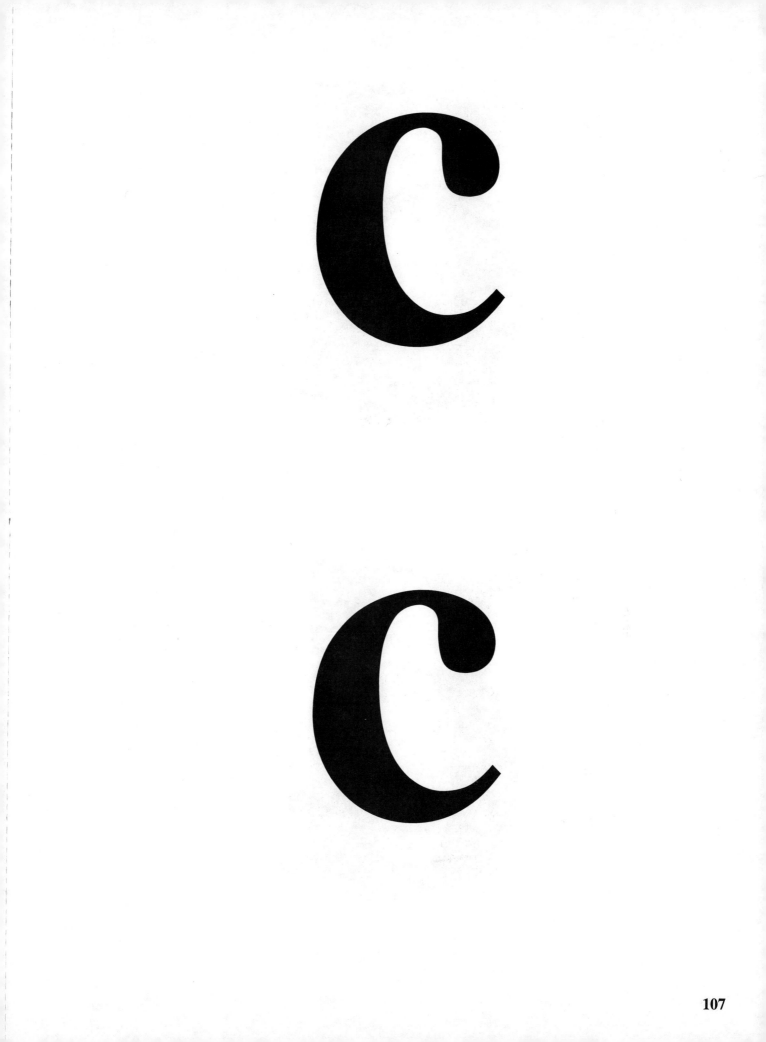

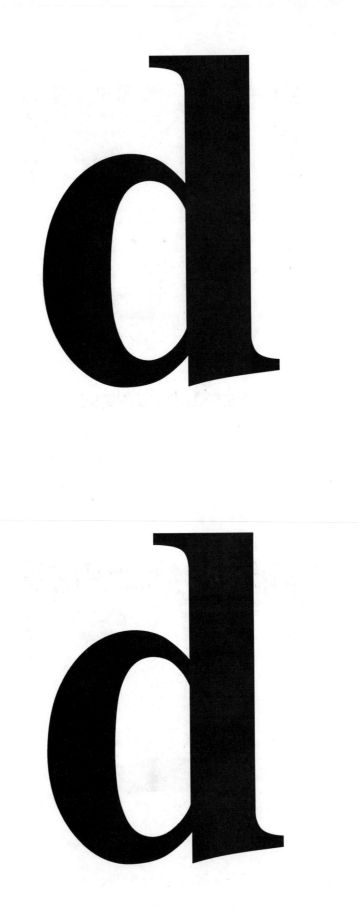

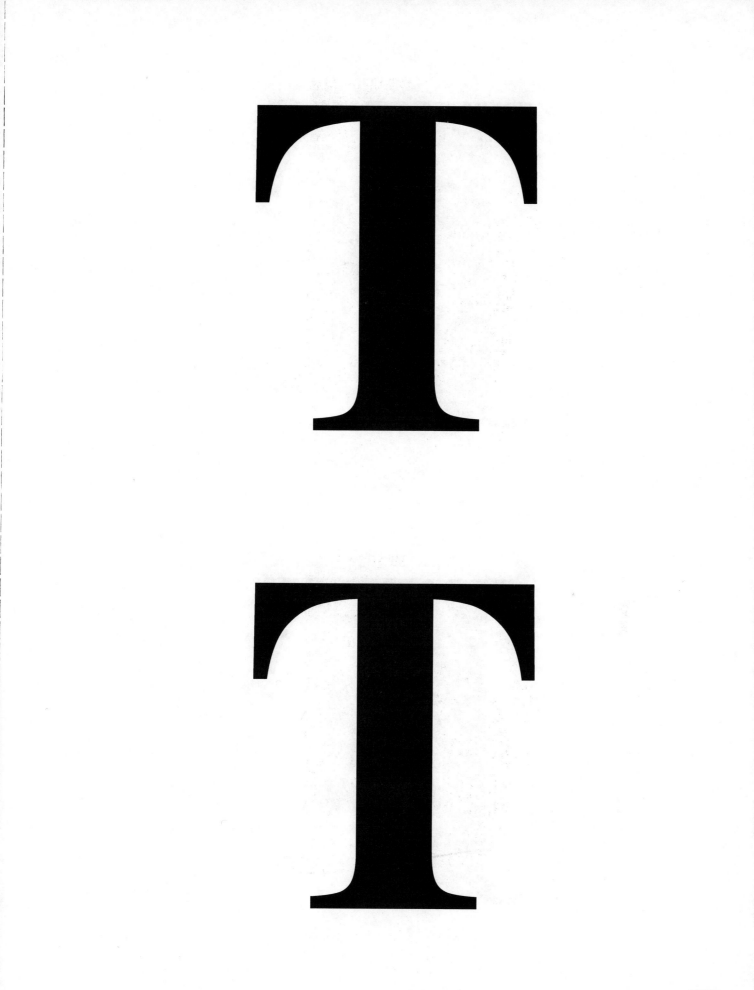

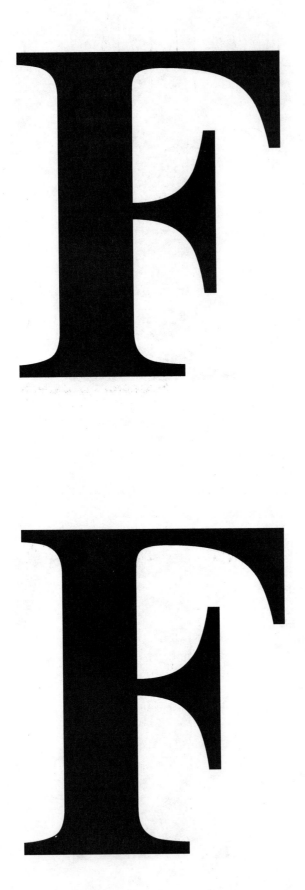

HUMAN CONTINUUM

Based on "Active Self-Assessment" in Silberman, M. (1995). *101 ways to make training active.* Johannesburg: Pfeiffer & Company, 209–210.

Goals: to help students understand themselves, their views, and why they hold the opinions they do

Group size: 10–50 students

Time required: 15–30 minutes

Materials: a large room and list of controversial statements

Physical setting: Participants are asked to imagine a continuum, with one wall of the room labeled the positive pole or "strongly agree" and the opposite wall labeled the negative pole or "strongly disagree."

Process: Read statements such as the ones listed below, based on course content. After each statement, ask participants to position themselves along the imaginary continuum formed between the two walls (poles). Ask students at various points to articulate why they are standing in a particular spot, such as a pole. Suggest they notice who is positioned close to them each time a new statement is read. Do they "travel" with the same few individuals? Does one other individual seem to share many of the same views? What are their perceptions of people at the opposite pole? Are they uncomfortable with "extreme" positions? Do they choose to stay in the middle? What does this exercise tell them about themselves?

"The United States should solve its own social problems before giving foreign aid to other countries."
"Same-sex marriages should be sanctioned by the state of _____."
"Students with learning disabilities really aren't equipped to handle college."
"AIDS research should be funded at a higher level than cancer research."
"The average student studies three hours outside class for every hour in class."
"Sex, drugs, and alcohol are the biggest problems on college campuses today."
"The most important role college plays is preparing students for the world of work."
"The Internet is a good place to meet romantic partners."

Variation: Additional statements may be created around course themes, current events, social issues, or typical freshman problems. If the group is large, ask for six or eight volunteers to demonstrate the exercise while others observe and discuss.

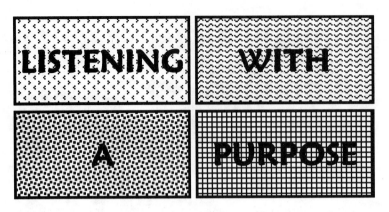

Based on "Listening Teams" in Silberman, M. (1995). *101 ways to make training active.*
Johannesburg: Pfeiffer & Company, 101–103.

Goals: to help students listen attentively to lectures and respond to course material

Group size: 12–40 participants optimal

Time required: lecture plus 20–40 minutes

Materials: none required

Physical setting: normal classroom in which participants are divided into four teams:

Team	Role	Assignment
1	Questioners	After the lecture is finished, ask two questions about the material.
2	Nay-Sayers	After the lecture is finished, comment on two points with which the group disagrees.
3	Yea-Sayers	After the lecture is finished, comment on two points with which the group agrees.
4	Explainers	After the lecture is finished, give two specific examples that explain the lecture.

Process: Before the lecture, give the teams their assignments. After the lecture, allow the teams to confer. Proceed from group to group, asking each team to do what you have requested. After all teams have finished, discuss listening skills with the entire group.

Variation: Additional roles may be created for variety or to demonstrate a particular principle.

Everyone's the Teacher

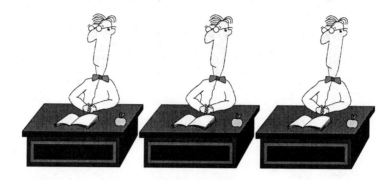

Based on "Everyone Is a Teacher Here" in Silberman, M. (1995). *101 ways to make training active*. Johannesburg: Pfeiffer & Company, 174–175.

Goals: to help students participate and to stress individual accountability

Group size: any size group

Time required: dependent on the size of the group

Materials: One index card per participant

Physical setting: normal class/training room

Process: Ask each participant to write one question on an index card following a lecture or discussion on a particular topic. Shuffle the cards and redistribute them. Ask participants to read their cards and think of an answer to their question. Ask volunteers to read their questions aloud and give a response. Ask the rest of the group to comment or add to the answer given. (Note: It's best to ask for volunteers. Some participants may have been given "impossible" or poorly written questions and be embarrassed that they cannot answer them.)

Variation: Create a panel of "experts" (and rotate/replace participants frequently to keep interest high).

WAKE-UP CALL

Based on "Lecture Letup" in Eitington, J. E. (1996).
The winning trainer (3rd edition). Houston: Gulf Publishing, 399.

GOALS: to help students listen to a lecture with full concentration

GROUP SIZE: any size class

TIME REQUIRED: exercise may last the length of the lecture

MATERIALS: give each student (or a representative group if the class is large) a numbered slip before beginning the lecture

PHYSICAL SETTING: a normal classroom setting or lecture hall

PROCESS: Set an electric timer to go off at five- or ten-minute intervals. When the timer goes off, call a random number (but keep track so that you don't repeat numbers). The student holding that number must 1) ask a question, 2) make a comment, or 3) summarize the last few minutes of content.

VARIATION: You may only want to try this exercise once at the beginning of the term to illustrate the importance of attentiveness. Done repeatedly, it could raise anxieties, but doing it once can be fun and have memorable results.

SOLVING THE CASE

Goals: to capture students' attention at the beginning of a lecture and to help them learn lecture material through application

Group size: any size class

Time required: the duration of the lecture

Materials: a written case study, or a script and actor(s)

Physical setting: any classroom setting

Process: Before beginning the lecture, pass out a written case study, indicating to students that at the conclusion of the lecture, they will use its content to "solve" the case. Allow the students time to read the case, and you may want to encourage them to discuss the case in small groups to identify what to listen for during the lecture. In some courses, it may even be more compelling to write a script for a skit to be acted out by you and a student or by two or more students as a visual case study. Again, indicate that the class will use the lecture material afterwards to analyze the case. At the conclusion of the lecture, ask students to work in groups, perhaps using a worksheet you construct, applying principles from the lecture to the problem presented in the case, followed by a general discussion.

Variation: Have students suggest scenarios for a written or visual case study the following week and choose the best one for class.

Note-Taking "Four-M"

1. **M**atching   **2. Missing**   **3. Meaning**   **4. Measuring**

Goals: to help first-year students take complete notes, process information, and test their listening comprehension

Group Size: any size group, including large lecture classes

Time Required: several 15-minute breaks during a long lecture

Materials: quiz questions on PowerPoint slides, transparencies, or paper

Physical Setting: normal classroom or lecture hall

Process: Stop a lecture periodically and ask each student to pair up with another student and engage in Steps 1 through 3:

Step 1. Compare notes they have taken from the previous portion of the lecture. Look for *matching* information, that is, sections where each student has written down the same thing.

Step 2. Look for *missing* pieces of information from either set of notes.

Step 3. Talk briefly about the *meaning* of the information, why it might have been included in the lecture, how it relates to past lectures, where the lecture might go next and so forth.

After you have given students a few minutes to complete these three steps, move to Step 4 by *measuring* their comprehension through a "Visible Quiz" on PowerPoint slides or a paper quiz so that they realize they will be accountable for what they have discussed with their partners. Many students are interactive learners, as opposed to auditory ones, and this exercise can greatly aid comprehension and learning. The "Visible Quiz" can also help you, as the lecturer, gauge and adjust your lecture pace or content level.

Variation: So that students get to know one another in large classes, suggest that they vary their partners and use the opportunity to meet as many classmates as possible over the term.

Finding the...

Fla✗✗✗✗w

Goals: to heighten students' listening skills during a lecture and to focus their attention on specific content.

Group size: any size group

Time required: the normal amount of time allotted to lecture

Materials: one index card per student

Physical setting: normal classroom or lecture hall setting

Process: Begin the lecture with an announcement such as the following: "Sometime during today's lecture, I will intentionally insert a piece of misinformation. Listen for it, and 'Find the Flaw.' When you hear it, make note of it on the index card I have given you. I will collect the cards as you leave class, and announce how many of you found the flaw successfully next week. Between now and then, see if you can find the correct information and bring it with you to next week's class session." You may also conduct the exercise verbally on the spot, by asking students to raise their hands when they think they have heard the inaccuracy. This may be a livelier format although with a highly spirited group, it holds the risk of totally derailing the lecture. The range of results will be interesting: some students will find the flaw easily and others, who are less engaged with the course content, will nominate perfectly accurate material. The point, of course, is to help students test their critical listening and critical thinking skills, and to challenge them to become more actively involved—to give them a *reason* to listen.

Variation: Instead of asking students to find an inaccuracy, begin the class session by announcing a preposterous proposition or a bizarre "What if?" question that will be examined during the lecture, one that will undoubtedly grasp students' attention and stimulate ensuing discussion.

Goals: to help students follow the intellectual course of a lecture and stay attuned by "filling in the blanks"

Group Size: any size class

Physical Setting: a large lecture hall or any classroom in which you are lecturing

Materials: a lecture map you create, citing the major principles you want students to master or factual details you would like them to absorb

Process: To a lecturer, the lecture makes perfect sense and integrates into a coherent whole. To students, however, information goes by quickly, and they may lack the intellectual infrastructure to "connect the conceptual dots." Instructors can help students process information readily by creating "lecture maps" that identify key points and asking students to fill in and process material. A map may list key points and ask for supporting evidence from the lecture, or you may design a "map" in which the lecture is divided into chunks, and ask students to process questions that follow each chunk, either individually or in small groups.

Variation: An infinite variety of potential maps can be created, depending on your purposes and the nature of your lecture. While this tool requires advance preparation time, it can free students up from the demand of continuous writing, encourage more discussion, and allow them to process information as it is delivered.

Skills-Based Exercises: Speaking, Writing, Technology

This section is intended to help students:

- **Learn technology at their own rate of competence and confidence.**

- **Understand the criteria for excellence in speaking and writing assignments.**

- **Find creative stimuli to use in practicing their speaking and writing skills.**

Goals: to help students organize their thoughts, present their ideas clearly, and generally hone their oral communication skills

Group size: any size class

Time required: any portion of normal class time

Materials: quotations, such as those on the following pages

Physical setting: any classroom setting; however, a U-shape or circle works well

Process: Cut the quotations on the following pages into strips (or create your own list of quotes). Have each student draw one and place it face down in front of him or herself. Choose a student volunteer to begin the exercise. He or she should turn over the slip, read the quotation, and offer a one-minute response by first agreeing or disagreeing with the quote and then identifying two pieces of support from personal experience, course material, or other relevant information sources. When one student begins to speak, the next student to speak may turn over his or her slip and begin formulating a response. If students seem anxious about speaking in front of classmates, reassure them that everyone will start on "equal footing" and reassert the value of learning to "speak on your feet."

Variation: Identify similar individual "quotations" from your lecture, or particular important points you plan to make, and hand them out on slips before you begin. Ask students to listen for their point, and after you conclude the lecture, to agree, disagree, or comment on the point they have been dealt. If the group is large, give slips to several volunteers or "Quotefinder" designees for the class session, instead of everyone.

Education

Education worthy of the name is essentially the education of character.   *Martin Buber*

Learning is what most adults will do for a living in the 21st century.   *Perelman*

If you think education is expensive, try ignorance.   *Derek Bok, president, Harvard University*

A teacher affects eternity.   He can never tell where his influence stops.   *Henry Brooks Adams, grandson of John Quincy Adams*

You should have education enough so that you won't have to look up to people; and then more education so that you will be wise enough not to look down on people.   *M. L. Boren*

Education is learning a lot about how little you know.   *Proverb*

Education is not filling a bucket but lighting a fire.   *William Butler Yeats*

Human history becomes more a race between education and catastrophe.   *H. G. Wells*

There are obviously two educations. One should teach us how to make a living and the other how to live.   *James Truslow Adams, American essayist & historian*

Education is the best provision for old age.   *Aristotle*

I attribute my success in life to the moral, intellectual and physical education which I received from my mother.   *George Washington*

Education should include knowledge of what to do with it.   *Unknown*

There was an educational channel in the good old days; it was called "off."   *Unknown*

It makes little difference how many university courses or degrees a person may own. If he cannot use words to move an idea from one point to another, his education is incomplete.   *Norman Cousins*

Education is what survives when what has been learned has been forgotten.   *B. F. Skinner*

It is regrettable for the education of the young that war stories are always told by those who survived.   *Louis Scutenaire*

Since we live in an age of innovation, a practical education must prepare a man for work that does not yet exist and cannot yet be clearly defined.   *Peter F. Drucker*

The educated differ from the uneducated as much as the living from the dead.   *Aristotle*

The aim of education should be to teach us rather how to think, than what to think—rather to improve our minds, so as to enable us to think for ourselves, than to load the memory with the thoughts of other men.   *James Beattie, Scottish poet*

We are by nature observers and thereby learners. That is our permanent state.   *Ralph Waldo Emerson*

Education worthy of the name is essentially the education of character.   *Martin Buber*

Education is the ability to listen to almost anything without losing your temper or your self-confidence.   *Robert Frost*

Life purpose
We live very close together. So, our prime purpose in life is to *help* others. And if you can't *help* them, at least don't *hurt* them.   *Dalai Lama*

We are all born for love. It is the principle of existence and its only end.   *British Prime Minister Benjamin Disraeli*

Life can only be understood backwards, but it must be lived forwards.   *Søren Kierkegaard*

Individual vs. group
Just remember, we're all in this alone.   *Lily Tomlin*

Hard work
I'm a great believer in luck, and I find the harder I work, the more I have of it.
Thomas Jefferson

Career
To love what you do and feel that it matters—how could anything be more fun?
Katherine Graham, publisher

Self-understanding
Knowing others is intelligence; knowing yourself is true wisdom. Mastering others is strength; mastering yourself is true power.   *Lao-Tzu*

The battles that count aren't the ones for gold medals. The struggles within yourself—the invisible, inevitable battles inside all of us—that's where it's at.   *Jessie Owens, winner of four gold medals at the 1936 Olympics*

Choice
Every choice we make allows us to manipulate the future.   *Captain Picard, Star Trek, the Next Generation*

Attitude

What you're supposed to do when you don't like a thing is change it. If you can't change it, change the way you think about it. Don't complain. *Advice to Maya Angelou from her Grandmother*

I learned many years ago that the genuinely happy people I meet are not happy because they have had only good fortune. I know that they are choosing their attitude. *Dr. Bernie Siegel*

People are about as happy as they make up their mind to be. *Abraham Lincoln*

Success

We were born to succeed not to fail. *Henry David Thoreau*

Success is the sum of small efforts, repeated day in and day out. *Robert Collier*

The measure of success is not whether you have a tough problem to deal with, but whether it's the same problem you had last year. *John Foster Dulles*

Success is not the key to happiness. Happiness is the key to success. If you love what you are doing, you will be successful. *Albert Schweitzer*

Always aim for achievement and forget about success. *Helen Hayes*

Mistakes vs. failure

A man may make mistakes, but he isn't a failure until he starts blaming someone else.
John Wooden

Failure is an opportunity to begin again more intelligently. *Henry Ford*

Challenge

Consider that people are like tea bags. They don't know their own strength until they get into hot water. *Dan McKinnon*

Dreams and goals

Always dream and shoot higher than you know you can do. Don't bother just to be better than your contemporaries or predecessors. Try to be better than yourself. *William Faulkner*

We are what we imagine ourselves to be. *Kurt Vonnegut*

If you don't dream, you may as well be dead. *George Foreman, oldest man to ever win the World Heavyweight Boxing Championship*

Goals are dreams with a deadline. *Anthony Robbins*

You are really never playing an opponent. You are playing yourself, your own highest standards, and when you reach your limits, that is real joy. *Arthur Ashe, tennis champion*

Time management
Time is the coin of your life. It is the only coin you have, and only you can determine how it will be spent. *Carl Sandburg*

Nothing is so fatiguing as the eternal banging of an uncompleted task. *William James*

Commitment to excellence
I just tried to make a habit to do the best I could.... I did that in school; I did it in the practice of law; and I did it in every job I've ever had. *Sandra Day O'Connor, Supreme Court Justice*

The Value of a Man's Life Is in Direct Proportion to His Commitment to Excellence. *Sign in Dallas Cowboys' locker room, attributed to Vince Lombardi*

We are what we repeatedly do. Excellence, then, is not an act, but a habit. *Aristotle*

It's a funny thing about life. If you refuse to accept anything but the best, you very often get it. *W. Somerset Maugham*

If we all did the things we are capable of doing, we would literally astound ourselves. *Thomas A. Edison*

Criticism
Honest criticism is hard to take, particularly from a relative, a friend, an acquaintance, or a stranger. *Franklin P. Jones*

PowerPoint Twelve-Point Exercise

Goals: to help students learn to use PowerPoint on their own, using an assignment handout and circulating instructor (no formal teaching)

Group Size: any number of students

Time Required: approximately 1–2 hours

Materials: ideally, a computer for each student with the latest version of PowerPoint installed; the handout on the following page

Physical Setting: a computer lab; however, the assignment may be done as homework instead

Process: Give each student a copy of the "PowerPoint Twelve-Point Exercise" sheet that follows. The assignment requires students to design an autobiographical PowerPoint slide show of 3–5 slides. In completing the assignment, students must check off twelve tasks that allow them to "play" with the software, explore on their own, and learn its capabilities, as you circulate around the room and answer questions. Formal teaching of software is difficult because students' capabilities vary a great deal, and those who already know the program will wander onto their favorite websites, check email, etc. Some students will have used PowerPoint frequently in high school, while others will never have heard of it. This activity allows students to work at their own pace; even students familiar with the program can learn more about its extensive capabilities.

Variation: As the course proceeds, require sequentially more challenging PowerPoint assignments so that students continue to hone their skills.

✓ ✓ ✓ ✓ ✓ ✓ ✓ ✓ ✓ ✓ ✓ ✓

First-Year Seminar

PowerPoint Twelve-Point Exercise

Name_____ Section_____

Assignment: Create a 3–5 slide PowerPoint presentation about yourself, your family, a hobby, or something that interests you to present to the class.

In creating your slide show, complete and check off the following tasks:

1._____ Change the **size**, **font**, **shadow**, and **color** of the wording on your title slide. Add a **sound effect** to the title slide only.

2._____ Create unusual **bullets** to include on one of your slides.

3._____ Make the **background** of each slide unique, but make sure the overall "package" has a color scheme that ties it together.

4._____ Incorporate **clip art** onto some of your slides. **Recolor** a piece of clip art so that it fits your presentation better.

5._____ Vary the **lines** and **fills** on your slides.

6._____ Play with the **order** of a section of text or graphics by putting one thing behind another.

7._____ **Rotate** a picture or some text.

8._____ Use a **design template** for one of your slides.

9._____ Minimize PowerPoint. Go into Internet Explorer. Right-click on a **graphic** you'd like to use in your presentation, copy it, minimize Internet Explorer, bring PowerPoint back up, and paste the graphic onto a slide. (This is also possible in Netscape Navigator, but it requires saving the file first as an intermediate step.)

10._____ Switch to the slide sorter mode of PowerPoint and choose **transitions** between each slide.

11._____ Format some custom **animations** so that portions of one or more slides (text or graphics) enter from different directions or move during your presentation.

12._____ Check your spelling, and view your slide show. Save it on a disk to bring to class, and make a **print copy** of your slides to hand in to your instructor, along with this checklist.

Critical Thinking--Critical Searching

Goals: to help students learn how to critique websites for academic use

Group size: any number of students

Time required: 45 minutes to one hour, or done outside of class as a homework assignment

Materials: a copy of the exercise that follows, including the website links and a comparison worksheet

Physical setting: computer lab, if done in class

Process: First-year students are often technologically proficient, more so than their parents or teachers, but they may know little about using technology productively in their academic work. In the assignment that follows, students are asked to compare four websites using seven criteria: 1) accuracy, 2) authority, 3) objectivity/perspective, 4) currency, 5) coverage/scope, 6) purpose, and 7) access. Discuss each of the criteria first, and then circulate and answer questions from individual students while they work.

Variation: Select websites based on the specific content of your course.

The Internet is an excellent tool that can help you conduct academic research for your classes. It can help you find facts quickly and relatively easily, but it's important to know how to navigate the sea of information you find and how to evaluate a site in terms of seven characteristics: 1) accuracy, 2) authority, 3) objectivity/perspective, 4) currency, 5) coverage/scope, 6) purpose, and 7) access.

Critical Thinking--Critical Searching

Assignment: Assume you have been asked to write a paper on the ethnic conflict in Bosnia for your Freshman Seminar class. From your browser, examine the four Websites below, looking for evidence in terms of the characteristics discussed. Fill in the chart below with your observations, and draw some conclusions about which sites you would use and why.

Website 1: www.unhcr.ba/
Website 2: www.cco.caltech.edu/~bosnia/bosnia.html
Website 3: www.friendsofbosnia.org
Website 4: www.applicom.com/twibih/

	Accuracy	Authority	Objectivity/ Perspective	Currency	Coverage/ Scope	Purpose	Access
1							
2							
3							
4							

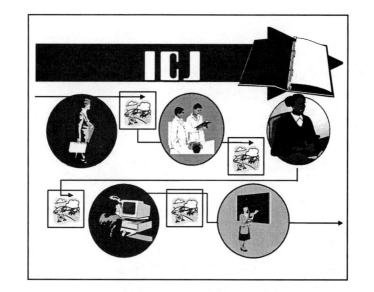

Internet Career Journey

(a technology-based activity based on the work of Barbara Gaddis and
Judith Rice-Jones at CU-Colorado Springs)

Goals: to help first-year students explore career options while learning to use the Internet as a research tool

Group Size: any size group (may easily be done as an out-of-class assignment)

Time Required: variable, depending on students' expertise and in-class vs. out-of-class format

Materials: one computer per student with Internet browser

Physical Setting: computer lab (or as homework)

Process: Ask students to research a potentially desirable career via the Internet. Their goal should be to build a portfolio that includes: 1) a printout or description of a career field of interest from the online *Occupational Outlook Handbook*, 2) a description of ten things they have learned about themselves and their career choices based on what they find, 3) a projection of their lifestyle twenty years into the future, including the career necessary to sustain that lifestyle, and other career-related factors of interest such as preparation required, necessary skills, additional training after college, pros and cons, entry salary range, advancement opportunities, personality characteristics of those in the career field, impact on family life, etc. Starting websites might include the following:

Occupational Outlook Handbook
   http://stats.bls.gov/oco/
Career Resource Center
   http://www.careers.org/

JobHunt
   http://www.job-hunt.org/
The Catapult on JobWeb
   http://www.jobweb.com/catapult/
The Riley Guide: Employment Opportunities and Job Resources on the Internet
   www.rileyguide.com
Monster.com
   http://www.monster.com/
Quintessential Careers
   http://www.quintcareers.com/index.html

Variation: Have students develop a "Webliography" of websites relevant to their career interests, rather than having you provide sites. It is also very useful to have students first complete on-line diagnostics that include career-related analyses such as the Keirsey Character Sorter found at http://keirsey.com.

The Good, the Bad, and the Ugly

Goals: to teach students via negative role modeling or flawed demonstrations

Group size: any size class

Time required: approximately 15 minutes

Materials: a PowerPoint presentation or web page design you have created to critique

Physical setting: a normal classroom setting or lecture hall with projection equipment

Process: Create a PowerPoint presentation that breaks all the rules you can think of:

The background is too busy to read the text.
The text is too small to read.
The font is illegible.
The color combinations are unattractive.
There is too much text per slide.
The sound effects become annoying.
The graphics have no relation to the text.
Excessive transitions and animations steal attention away from the message.

It is especially fun if the presentation is about you: "A Day in the Life of Professor X." You might elect to start with well-constructed slides that progressively break the rules until the effects are humorous. Ask the students to help you critique the presentation as you go—including the good, the bad, and the ugly. Today's students respond well to visual demonstrations, as opposed to verbal descriptions. A picture is still worth 1000 words!

Variation: Try writing a paper deliberately filled with flaws and ask the students to help you grade it.

What's in an A?

Goals: to help students identify the criteria by which speaking and writing assignments are graded and thereby strive for peak performance

Group size: individual work, followed by comparisons across small groups of four or five participants

Time required: approximately one hour

Materials: several student papers (with names removed) from previous terms (to focus on writing) and videotapes of past student speeches, if available (to focus on speaking), and copies of the criteria sheets (blank or filled in) that follow

Physical setting: normal classroom setting

Process: The exercise should be done separately for speaking and writing, or you may focus on both skills during one extended session. If you begin with speaking, for example, ask students to help you generate criteria upon which grades for student speeches are based in the far-left column of the blank criteria handout. They may list categories such as:

--topic selection	--organization
--thesis (clarity and organization)	--language use
--supporting material (evidence)	--delivery

If this seems too challenging (for example, they have never had a public speaking course in high school), you may use the sheet with criteria already filled in. After students create their own matrix, ask them to compare their criteria in small groups. As you work through the speaking criteria, ask participants to independently grade the videotaped speeches and then compare their grades, indicating which criteria they used and their relative value in assigning a grade. Or complete the exercise in similar fashion using the sample essays. Students enjoy "playing teacher," and the opportunity to view the process from "the other side" can be productive and motivating.

Variation: Generate the criteria yourself or use the exact ones published by your institution's Freshman Composition Program, Writing Center, or Speech Department.

Criteria for Grading Papers

Criteria	Excellent	Good	Average	Poor	Unsatisfactory
Purpose					
Ideas and development					
Audience awareness					
Focus and organization					
Syntax and style					
Grammar, usage, and mechanics					
General comments					

Criteria for Grading Papers

Criteria	Excellent	Good	Average	Poor	Unsatisfactory

Criteria for Grading Speeches

Criteria	Excellent	Good	Average	Poor	Unsatisfactory
Topic: important, appropriate, and focused?					
Thesis: clear and communicated?					
Support: Appropriate, accurate, and enough?					
Organization: clear, correct, and communicated?					
Language: appropriate, grammatical, and clear?					
Voice: varied, paced well, volume good?					
Delivery: animated, spontaneous, energetic?					
Intro/conclusion: rapport-building and memorable?					

Criteria for Grading Speeches

Criteria	Excellent	Good	Average	Poor	Unsatisfactory

Goals: to help students think creatively, organize their thoughts quickly, present their ideas persuasively, and generally hone their oral communication skills

Group size: any size class

Time required: any portion of normal class time

Materials: a shopping bag filled with common objects from your office, kitchen, etc.

Physical setting: any classroom setting

Process: Ask student volunteers to draw an object out of the shopping bag (without looking) and give the class a one-minute sales pitch. The catch, however, is that they must find a new use for the item. For example, a student who draws an egg slicer might sell it as a "pocket guitar."

Variation: Ask students to bring unusual objects to class for the exercise. Or do the activity as a team-based task. Give each group of 4–5 students a bag of junk. Ask them to create something as a team and sell it to the class.

GOALS: to help students organize their thoughts quickly, present their ideas dynamically, and generally hone their oral communication skills

GROUP SIZE: any size class

TIME REQUIRED: any portion of normal class time

MATERIALS: a newspaper rolled up into a cylindrical shape

PHYSICAL SETTING: any classroom setting

PROCESS: Ask student volunteers to give a one-minute speech on a pet peeve or something that really makes them angry: tailgating, getting a ticket, running out of gas, finding the website they need "down" for maintenance, getting into the slow line at the store, etc. As they speak, they should hit the side of the lectern or the desk at the front of the room with the newspaper from time to time for emphasis. (Warn students not to offend others with their language, if you think this could become an issue.)

VARIATION: Ask students to write down their ideas on index cards, choose the best ones for class use, and allow students to draw a card rather than select their own topic.

Discipline-Specific Exercises

Activities in this section were contributed by guest authors/teachers from a variety of disciplines. Some can be readily adapted to other disciplines as well.

All Disciplines

Art History

Astronomy/Physics

Chemistry

College Success/First-Year Experience

Communication

Composition and Rhetoric

Film Studies

Geography

Humanities

Literature

Guest Author: Barbara J. Millis, U.S. Air Force Academy, with special thanks to Steve Sugar, the Game Group

Discipline: English with applications in virtually any discipline

Goals: This activity, a replication of a BINGO game, works wonderfully to involve students in a review of course material. Because students generate different types of questions for the game, it also gets them thinking not only about factual questions related to the discipline, but also about higher-order questions. Since the students become the experts responsible for the questions they generate, they also benefit from acquiring the deep learning that enables them to teach the subject matter to their peers.

Besides the active involvement with learning, the assessment value of QUIZO/BINGO is extremely valuable. When students submit the questions, I get an immediate sense of their knowledge, and they get feedback on the quality and fairness of their questions. As the question experts, they teach the material, making the class student-centered. After the game ends, I can review the worksheets with the recorded answers to get a sense of which questions students missed or did well on. Best of all, students are energetic and enthusiastic, "high-fiving" each other when they get a correct answer. They listen attentively to the answers and suddenly care about the material, even where the commas go in an MLA bibliography entry!

Group size: QUIZO/BINGO is best played with small classes, 25 or under. However, I have used it in faculty workshops with over 80 participants, so it is "doable" with larger groups.

Time required: I usually conduct a QUIZO/BINGO game in a 50-minute class time, although I wish for more time. Things are pretty rushed without as much time for discussion of complex questions as I would wish. A 90-minute class period would probably be ideal.

QUIZO/BINGO involves a fair amount of up-front preparation time, primarily cutting and pasting the questions and answers into two formats: (1) large-font questions and answers (one per transparency) for use in class, and (2) a composite of all questions and answers to be used as a study guide. This composite can be distributed in class following play, sent to students via email, or posted to a class website. Students submit their questions electronically at least two days prior to the day of play.

Materials:

Instructors will need QUIZO/BINGO game sheets on which to place the markers when students answer questions correctly. These can purchased as part of a commercial set from The Game Group, 10320 Kettledrum Court, Ellicott City, MD 21042 (Phone Steve Sugar: 410-418-4930). Or, you can create your own game sheets using the table feature on common software packages such as Word or WordPerfect.

Instructors also need a way for students to determine which square on their game sheets the markers will go. I have used a variety of options, all of which determine the letter—Q U I Z O, in my classes—and the number under that letter, 1–5. For the letters, I have used scrabble markers, sets of letters purchased in variety stores, homemade squares, or poker chips marked with the letters. For the numbers, I either use a regular die which students re-throw if a six emerges or a special ten-sided die with only five numbers, which I purchased in a novelty store. The commercial set from the Game Group provides prepared cards with both the letter and the number.

Students need worksheets on which to record their answers so that they can see their progress, so that you can verify their win, and most importantly, so that you can see how well prepared each student pair appears to be for the midterm exam or the final.

Students need markers to place on each square, and of course, prizes for the first pairs to reach "QUIZO/BINGO" as incentives. I purchase needed supplies: Skittles or M&Ms for the QUIZO/BINGO markers (seasonal variations can be Halloween candy corn or Valentine hearts), and candy bars—large and snack sizes—for the prizes. Other possible prizes can include small Kleenex packs, pens, cocoa packets, highlighters, etc—whatever appeals to your students.

Physical setting:

A classroom with desk or table space is essential. Students need space to work in pairs with a hard surface to lay out their QUIZO/BINGO game sheets and worksheets.

Process:

Prior to playing, I ask students to send me electronically two questions and answers, one factual and one involving higher-order thinking. In ENGL 111, for example, the latter questions would ask classmates to complete a bibliographic entry. In the literature class, they would respond to a question involving interpretation (e.g., Why did Antigone insist on burying her brother?). If students submit misleading, inaccurate, or awkwardly constructed question-answer sets, I ask them to rethink and then resubmit. I compile the questions by category (factual/higher order) and arrange them in the order I want them introduced into play. I also add any significant questions I feel should be included. I then prepare transparencies with enlarged fonts that give the question and the person submitting it. The answer, including, if appropriate, the page reference, appears below on the same transparency page, with plenty of empty space above so I can easily cover it during play.

To play the game, I pair students (weaker with stronger students for better coaching and teaching) and explain the procedure. Each pair gets markers and different colored worksheets (green for the factual; gold for the higher-level questions) where they record their answers and if they were right or wrong. I pose the questions in sequence within each category, giving sufficient time based on their complexity. The student who submitted the question is the expert/arbitrator who decides what alternative answers are acceptable.

Pairs with correct answers place a marker on the designated square (e.g., Q2 or Z4). The square is determined by having the pairs in turn draw a scrabble letter or its equivalent (Q,U,I,Z,O) and roll a die. I use the factual questions to speed up play and use the higher-order thinking questions for class discussion/teaching.

The first pair (often there will be ties) to cover five contiguous squares in any direction declares "QUIZO." They then clear their board and continue playing until the period ends. In a 50-minute period, I try to have every pair become "winners." The winners pick their prizes, with those scoring first having the choice of the larger candy bars. As a follow-up, I give each student a copy of the questions and answers to use as a study guide.

Variation: Because QUIZO/BINGO already fosters a variety of goals—acquisition of content knowledge, motivation, student involvement, generation of a study guide, assessment for both students and teachers—I cannot think of additional ones. I would like to emphasize, however, that this highly interactive activity is effective for any discipline and for virtually any type of learner.

Send/Pass-a-Problem

Guest Author: Barbara J. Millis, U.S. Air Force Academy

Discipline: English, with applications in other disciplines

Goals: This activity encourages critical problem solving because students in groups brainstorm creative solutions to given problems within a discipline and then compare them with alternative solutions generated by other teams. Virtually all of the research literature on critical thinking emphasizes the need to consider alternative viewpoints. This activity also encourages higher-order thinking because students are evaluating the input from other teams and consciously synthesizing alternative viewpoints for the optimum solution to the given problem. Evaluation and synthesis appear at the highest level of Bloom's well-known taxonomy. Additionally, the group work involved in Send/Pass-a-Problem enhances teamwork skills and encourages students to value the input of others.

I use Send/Pass-a-Problem in my English classes for literary interpretations that must be supported by textual evidence. Because students dig into the texts, doing the actual work rather than passively listening to canned lectures, they learn far more.

Send/Pass-a-Problem works well not only from a critical-thinking perspective, but also because the novelty of passing folders/boxes, creatively brainstorming, and comparing ideas gets students actively involved with the course material.

Group size: With careful planning, this activity can be conducted with any number of students. The minimum number of students would be six to nine, the maximum in the hundreds.

Time required: The time required will depend on the complexity of the problems and the size of the classes. In my English class, composed of approximately 20 students, I can complete a Send/Pass-a-Problem activity within the 50-minute class period, including report-outs. In larger classes, report-outs would need to be posted by a group recorder to a web page or circulated via e-mail. Another alternative is to conclude the class with an active report-out method called a Gallery Walk. A Gallery Walk requires a report-out that can be visually depicted, preferably on butcher paper. It can be an outline, a concept or mind map, or any other written product. Usually a designated student stays by the desk or table or next to the butcher paper if it is taped to the wall and serves as the group spokesperson. The other students rotate around the room examining the products of other teams' thinking, asking questions of the designated spokesperson. (The spokesperson role should be rotated so that no one is left without the stimulation of exploring the different student creations.) In the case of a Send/Pass-a-Problem, a spokesperson may not be necessary so long as the problem is clearly posted to the wall with the synthesized solution.

Materials: Instructors need to bring blank file folders for student-selected problems (see explanation below) or prelabeled file folders for teacher-selected problems. (Envelopes, boxes, or any other item suitable for rotation can be used in place of file folders.) Each team will need blank sheets of paper or prepared worksheets on which to record their solutions.

Physical setting: Students need a work surface or clipboards to record their ideas. Teams need to be able to put their heads together during the activity, but virtually any classroom setting, including auditoriums, can work, provided the logistics are well thought out in advance.

Process: The exact source of this problem-solving activity is unknown. The Howard County Maryland Staff Development Center developed a version of it inspired by Kagan's (1989)[1] work. The starting point is a list of problems or issues, which can be generated by students or can be teacher-selected. In a student-selected scenario with smaller classes, each team identifies the particular problem or issue on which they wish to focus initially and records their choice on the front of a folder. Each team selects a different problem. In larger classes, only three different problems are needed, provided they are spaced appropriately so that each individual team works on the three different problems. Thus, folders can be pre-prepared and brought to class.

Once teams have a folder with the problem identified on the cover, they then brainstorm effective solutions for these problems and write them down on a piece of paper or special worksheet. At a predetermined time, the ideas are placed in the folder and forwarded to another team. The members of the second team, without looking at the ideas already generated, compile their own solutions. This second set of ideas is forwarded to a third team which now looks at the suggestions provided by the other two teams, adds its own, and then works on a synthesis of all three teams' best thinking. Some faculty members

---

[1] Kagan, S. (1989). *Cooperative learning.* San Juan Capistrano, CA: Resources for Teachers.

use this structure for examination review sessions by putting typical exam questions in folders for group problem solving.

Variation: The goals will vary from discipline to discipline. ESL or foreign language courses, for example, may seek to increase motivation and fluency by having students in teams create captions for captionless cartoons in the target language. The final evaluation involves not only the most humorous response, but also the most fluently worded one. This versatile activity can involve students in working through accounting or math problems, identifying characteristics of rocks or plants (passed in boxes) in biology or botany classes, or having prelaw or paralegal students annotate various professional journals. A geography course, such as the one taught by Captain Ken Hart at the U.S. Air Force Academy, might concentrate on in-depth understanding by focusing on questions such as: What makes the Balkan region unique as compared to other shatter belts? Discuss the relationship between the pattern of landforms and cultural diversity in Eastern Europe. Describe the physiography and climate of Southeast Asia and impact of population in the region.

In my English classes, I have used Send/Pass-a-Problem to explore literary interpretations such as why Hamlet treats Ophelia as he does: Hamlet is trying to protect her, Hamlet is a "jerk," etc. Teams are expected to provide textual support for their conclusions.

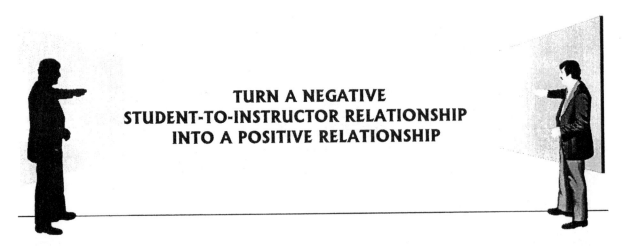

TURN A NEGATIVE
STUDENT-TO-INSTRUCTOR RELATIONSHIP
INTO A POSITIVE RELATIONSHIP

Guest Author: Timothy L. Walter, Oakland Community College
Discipline: All Disciplines

Goal: This exercise is designed to help students see how their attitudes and behaviors affect the performance of their instructors. Equally important is that we want students to understand how a negative attitude toward a course may result in them not only disliking the course, but learning very little. This exercise teaches students that by taking responsibility for thinking and behaving in positive ways toward their instructor and the course as a whole, they will find that they not only enjoy the course much more but also learn a lot.

We have always been very candid with students and discuss the fact that students need to accept that they will have great instructors, mediocre instructors, and some who are less than desirable. We suggest to students that their behavior in the classroom has a dramatic impact on their instructor's performance. The student can choose to behave in ways that result in better instructor performance, which in turn results in a more enjoyable learning experience. In contrast, the student can choose to behave in ways that cause instructors to teach poorly, be unhelpful, be boring, and have a distaste for teaching a class.

Another important insight for students is that students who don't appear to care about the course often create instructors that carry a chip on their shoulders. We say to the students, "The choice is yours. Figure out what behaviors you can display in class that will make the class more enjoyable for you. Ask yourself what you can consistently do in class to enhance your instructor's performance and make the class more enjoyable for you. We want you to see the relationship between your behavior and your instructor's performance. We want you to see the relationship between your attitude toward the class and how well you like the class and how much you learn."

We have used this exercise for better than 30 years. Students enjoy the exercise because they are able to talk about what it is that they like and dislike about courses. They can compare and contrast their likes and dislikes. As students carry out the project, they record their results and discuss them in class. This is a great exercise to get students talking to one another and to help them recognize the responsibility they must take for receiving a good education.

Group Size: This exercise has worked well in classes ranging from 15 to 150 students.

Time Required: The time required is essentially that of introducing the exercise in one of the first class sessions and then creating time on several occasions during the semester for students to discuss their results in class as often as you wish.

Materials Required: copies of the "Action Project" handout

Physical Setting: any classroom

Process: The activity is introduced to the students in one of the first class sessions. We have introduced this exercise in a variety of courses in psychology and education. It is also an excellent activity for a freshman orientation or freshman-year experience course.

We introduce the activity by asking students to first read the project. We avoid lecturing to them about negative influences students can have on an instructor's performance. Rather, we try to get them to look at the project as one in which they take responsibility for their education.

The project lends itself to class discussion. We typically ask the class as a group to walk through the steps of the project and answer the following questions:

"What behaviors do you see students exhibit in class which might result in instructors developing a negative attitude toward the class or an individual student? Can you give some examples of student behavior you have seen in your first few days in classes this semester that had a negative impact? Did you notice any particular effects on the instructor when the student/s acted this way?"

"Why do you think students act this way? Do you think they consciously do these things?"

"In contrast, if you were an instructor, what type of behaviors would you expect to see from students in a college course?"

"As a group, list all the things you could do in your courses that would result in your instructors teaching better and you enjoying and learning more from your course."

Once the students have developed answers to these questions, assign the project as one they will carry out over the semester. It is critical that students receive credit for the project. Dependent upon how much class time you have to devote to such a project, it is important that students be asked to write up, using the form, exactly what they intend to do in a specific class. We typically take class time to do this. Dependent upon the number of students, we often go around the room and ask students to identify one thing they will do in the class they have chosen. Although it would be ideal if the students demonstrated this new behavior in every class, we have found that it is best for them to focus on just one class. If the behavior pays off, they will generalize their actions to all of their classes.

We ask the students to carry out the project for several weeks and set a date to report back in class on Steps 3 and 4. In this class session, about a month later, the students can begin to reflect on:

"How has your behavior affected your instructor? Did you notice any changes in his or her behavior when you did these things? How did the instructor respond to you?"

"As you changed your behavior, what effects did this have on your attitude toward the class and how much you felt you were learning?"

"Have you noticed whether any of the other students in your class have started to model your behavior?"

This update session, about a month later, can be followed by a second update about two-thirds of the way through the semester. At the end of the semester, the students are asked to write-up the project in a narrative form using the information they collect via the four steps on the "Action Project" sheet. We have found that it is useful to have them describe their project in a short story of two pages or less. Students enjoy reflecting on what they have learned about the impact they can have on their instructor's performance. Equally important, they enjoy talking about how changing their behavior enhanced their own attitude toward the course and their learning.

Variation: One can vary this project by adapting it to any setting, such as the workplace, the home, or any social setting. The critical factor is getting people to see how by choosing to behave in more productive ways, they influence other people in positive ways and build stronger relationships.

ACTION PROJECT

Turn a Negative Instructor-to-Student Relationship into a Positive One

STEP 1. WHAT BEHAVIORS OR HABITS DO YOU EXHIBIT IN A CLASS YOU DON'T PARTICULARLY CARE FOR THAT MIGHT RESULT IN YOUR INSTRUCTOR DEVELOPING A NEGATIVE ATTITUDE TOWARD YOU? LIST THEM BELOW:

_____
_____
_____
_____

STEP 2. WHAT COULD YOU DO INSTEAD TO DRAW MORE POSITIVE REACTIONS TOWARD YOU? LIST THE BEHAVIORS BELOW:

_____
_____
_____
_____

STEP 3. PRACTICE YOUR NEW BEHAVIORS FOR A MONTH, THEN RETURN TO THIS SPACE AND DESCRIBE HOW YOUR BEHAVIOR HAS CHANGED IN THE CLASS. DISCUSS WHETHER OR NOT BY BEHAVING DIFFERENTLY YOU HAVE DEVELOPED A DIFFERENT ATTITUDE TOWARD THE CLASS AND THE INSTRUCTOR. WRITE YOUR ANSWER BELOW:

_____
_____
_____
_____

STEP 4. IF YOUR BEHAVIOR IN A CLASS CHANGED, DID YOUR PERCEPTION OF THE CLASS CHANGE? WHAT DOES THIS TELL YOU ABOUT THE EFFECTS OF YOUR HABITS ON YOUR ATTITUDES? WRITE YOUR ANSWER BELOW:

_____
_____
_____
_____

Wearable Art

Guest Author: Kathryn Andrus, University of Colorado at Colorado Springs

Discipline: Art History

Goals: This activity functions as an icebreaker (at the beginning of any course in Fine Arts), allowing for introductions and conversation, as well as an initiation to course objectives, art historical vocabulary, and ways to analyze and describe works of art.

Group size: The activity works best with a small to medium-sized group (20–25)

Time required: 10–15 minutes, longer if desired

Materials: Color reproductions of works of art (from the Internet, old posters, etc.), pencils or pens, index cards, and tape

Physical setting: This may be done in a classroom of any kind, but the students should be able to move about freely.

Process: Without letting students see the image, tape one to the back of each student. Students then introduce themselves to each other by soliciting a descriptive adjective from other students that describes the art illustrated in the reproduction on their back, which they can't see. They make a list of these adjectives. Students should be cautioned not to reveal the name of the artist or the title of the work, and each student should only offer one adjective. At the end of the interaction period, each student uses these words to guess the name of his or her work of art.

Variation: This activity may also be used to review for exams or to simply stimulate a sleepy class!

Cooperative Learning in Large General Astronomy Lectures

Guest Author: Tom Christensen, University of Colorado at Colorado Springs
Discipline: Astronomy/Physics

Goals: The primary goal of any educational endeavor should be to improve student learning. The concept that students learn well from one another (cooperative learning or peer instruction) is well established in both astronomy ["Interactive Lesson Guide for Astronomy: Cooperative Learning Activities," Michael Zeilik (The Learning Zone, Inc., Santa Fe, NM, 1998)] and in physics ["Peer Instruction: A User's Manual," Eric Mazur (Prentice Hall, Upper Saddle River, NJ, 1997)]. Cooperative learning can be implemented easily in large, introductory, lecture classes both to teach specific scientific concepts as well as to teach the process of doing science. The advantages of using these techniques have been discussed in the literature, but, in surveys I have given my general astronomy students, they express the advantages better than I could. I have arbitrarily grouped student comments into several key areas to identify some of the advantages of using cooperative learning exercises in large lecture classes.

1. Improved learning environment:
    "I thought the projects were very helpful and really helped to bring together a very
        large group of people, making the class more intimate."
    "Group activities kind of make the class go by quicker, and it is a good change of pace."

2. Active learning:
    "The projects helped me to understand the material and work hands on."
    ". . . gets people involved."

3. Multiple assessment methods:
    "These projects were a great way to help people like me that do not test so well!"

4. Multiple learning styles:
    "Allows people to learn things from each other."
    "You can get input and different perspectives working with others."
    "Get to learn things visually (with graphs) and work through problems."

An improved learning environment, active learning, multiple means of assessment and teaching to multiple learning styles are all recognized as good teaching pedagogy. Next, I will address the connection between this improved pedagogy and whether the students actually seem to change their behaviors and their understanding of concepts.

Students were surveyed on several issues. I began these surveys in semesters before I introduced the in-class cooperative learning exercises in order to establish a baseline. The number of students who never talked to other students about the course content declined from 25% to 5% when I introduced these exercises. Only about 7% of the students said that the process of discussing the material with other students did not help them in understanding the concepts.

In addition to the student comments and surveys, I also examined changes in test scores. I repeated a number of multiple-choice questions from midterm exams on the final exam. I selected questions from four topic areas that had been covered in cooperative learning exercises and three topic areas that were covered only in lecture. Those topics that were only covered in lecture typically showed slight decreases or slight increases in student performance. All of the topics that were included in cooperative learning exercises showed much larger increases in student performance with some topics having twice as many students answering the question correctly on the final exam.

Although the student reports and test results were very encouraging, what really excites me about this method of teaching is what I did while the students were working on these exercises. I wandered around the room and listened and consulted. This gave me a chance to actually hear my students think. That seldom happens in a lecture environment. It has given me a much greater understanding of why certain topics were confusing to students and has changed the way I lecture on those topics.

It is also important to recognize that some students will see these exercises as a disadvantage. Again from student comments:
> "It is too hard to work with others when we all think differently."
> "I learn more from lectures."
> "Someone in a group always slacks."

The instructor should be prepared to address these issues.

In summary, the use of these in-class cooperative learning exercises helps teach students both the concepts and processes of science. Test scores improve and self-reported student understanding increases. The instructor gets very direct feedback by listening to the students as they work out the problems. Pedagogically, these exercises help the instructor to teach using a more varied and interesting learning environment, addressing multiple learning styles in an active manner, and providing multiple means of assessment of student understanding.

Group size: These cooperative learning exercises can be done with any size class from threee students up to hundreds. I have worked with classes of 60–90 students in a lecture hall environment. Students can be divided into groups of three or four by having students in alternate rows turn around and work with the students immediately behind them.

Time required: I typically allow the students 20–30 minutes for each exercise. Based on survey results, the students preferred to have one exercise every other week. As a result, I gave up 4 hours of lecture during the semester to do these exercises. In some cases I simply reduced the amount of lecture on content that I was covering in the exercises. In other cases, I cut out material from the lecture that was probably marginally important anyway. I did not find any particular evidence that the class suffered particularly from losing 4 hours of inspiring lectures!

Materials: For each exercise, I handed out a photocopied exercise to each student. The students needed either a pen or pencil to fill out the exercise. Sometimes it was helpful to have a straight edge of some sort (like the cover of a notebook) to be able to draw a straight line on a graph.

Physical setting: These exercises can work in almost any environment. My classes were in a large lecture hall with swiveling chairs and permanent tables that ran all the way across the room. Labs or rooms with movable seating would also work well.

Process: After brief instructions from me on how the process works, students divided up into groups of three or four students. I typically began these exercises 20–30 minutes before the end of class. The exercise handout began with a paragraph that described the general topic area to be studied. Students were then asked to predict some type of result based on their knowledge of the subject. The exercise then led them through a series of questions that would bring them to understand the correct result of whatever they were asked to predict. Often these questions would include graphing actual data and drawing conclusions from the graph. Students were allowed to hand in their own work, although they were asked to indicate if they disagreed with their group's consensus. (They usually learned after a couple lessons that the group was more likely to get it right than any one individual.)

Variation: The exercises can be developed to work toward an understanding of almost any topic area. It may take a few iterations to get the level right so as to challenge the students without overwhelming them.

Enhancing Conceptual Understanding of Organic Chemistry with Collaborative Teams

Guest Authors: Barbara Gaddis and Allen Schoffstall, University of Colorado at Colorado Springs

Discipline: Chemistry

Goals: Electrophilic aromatic substitution is an important type of reaction in organic chemistry. Mastery involves conceptual understanding of Lewis structures, covalent bonding, formal charges, resonance, and potential energy diagrams. However, too often, students try to memorize reactions without understanding the underlying concepts. As a result, their learning is superficial at best.

Part of the problem is caused by the instructional methodologies typically used in science courses. Science teaching in the United States tends to be largely lecture-driven and students rely on professors to tell them what they need to learn. Students try to be successful by memorizing everything that the professor says and writes on the blackboard. As a result, many students do not develop the reasoning or critical-thinking skills that are necessary in a complex science like organic chemistry. Active learning strategies, on the other hand, force students to develop their own conceptual understanding about important scientific principles. With a firmer grounding in theory, students are better able to apply the concepts toward new problems rather than just trying to regurgitate memorized information. This exercise forces students to use their knowledge of covalent bonding and structure to construct the important concepts of electrophilic aromatic substitution.

Group size: Any number of students can be accommodated. This exercise has been performed in small classes of twenty-five students as well as in much larger classes. Each student first works individually on a series of problems. Each student is assigned one or more of the problems. Next the students collaborate in informal groups of 2–4 students to compare answers, to deduce trends, and ultimately to correlate structure to reactivity.

Time required: The time is variable depending upon the depth to which the topic of electrophilic aromatic substitution is to be taught. Approximately 15–60 minutes is needed depending upon the number of individual problems assigned to each student. Professors could choose to do part of the exercise or spend an entire lecture period developing the concepts of electrophilic aromatic substitution.

Materials: No special materials are necessary. Structures can either be written on the chalkboard or may be handed out in a worksheet. The worksheet is available at http://www.uccs.edu/~amschoff/chemexercise.html.

Physical setting: The exercise can be done using pencil and paper or a chalkboard. It can also be done by a group of students seated around a computer.

Process: Each student receives a worksheet showing partial structures of a variety of substituted aromatic compounds. The compounds are aniline, anisole, phenol, N-methylaniline, phenyl acetate, nitrobenzene, cyanobenzene, trifluoromethylbenzene, anilium chloride, toluene, benzoic acid, and benzenesulfonic acid. Students are told to complete drawings of the Lewis structures of the compounds. For example, for phenol (C6H5 – OH) students would add two pairs of electrons to the oxygen atom and for aniline (C6H5 – NH2), students would draw in one pair of electrons. Then students assign formal charges, partial positive charges, or partial negative charges to the atoms directly bonded to the aromatic ring.

Following completion of the worksheet, students are assigned to informal groups of 2–4 students. Teams are asked to examine the structures carefully and then to categorize the structures into two groups so that all members of the categories have similar structures. SWorking together, the team discovers that the structures can be classified based upon partial charges on the atom bonded to the ring: in one category all of the atoms have partial positive or full positive charges, while in the other category all of the atoms have partial negative charges. Many of the compounds in this latter group also have lone pairs of electrons on the atom bonded to the ring. After the students classify the structures, the professor reveals that the first group of compounds is called "deactivating," while the latter group of compounds is designated as "activating." These terms are not yet defined, but are simply used as category names. Students are then presented with several new substituted aromatic compounds and are asked to predict whether the substituents will be activating or deactivating. Having learned the relationship between structure and reactivity, students can easily determine the correct assignment.

Next, students analyze the concepts of reactivity. Students draw all resonance forms for the intermediates formed in the reaction of an electrophile with phenol (which has an activating substituent) for ortho-, meta-, and para-attack of the electrophile. Students are asked to identify resonance structures that are particularly stable or particularly unstable. Students repeat this process with nitrobenzene (which has a deactivating substituent). Again students identify resonance forms that are particularly stable and particularly unstable.

After writing resonance forms, students discover that ortho- and para-attack on phenol generates four resonance structures while meta-attack generates only three. The additional resonance structure is possible in ortho- and para- attack because the atom bonded to the ring can donate electron density into the ring. Meta-attack of the electrophile generates only three resonance structures. Based upon these results, students learn that activating substituents, having partial negative charges and/or lone pairs of electrons, can help stabilize the intermediate carbocation in ortho/para attack. Conversely, students discover when drawing resonance structures for nitrobenzene that ortho- and para-attack generate a particularly unstable intermediate, whereas meta-attack avoids placing a positive charge on an atom that is already partially positive. Comparing the stabilities of the intermediates with those generated by electrophilic attack on benzene, students can see that the intermediates formed with an activating substitutent are more stable and lower energy than the intermediate formed with benzene, while the intermediates formed with a deactivating substituent are less stable than those formed with benzene.

Based upon these results, students recognize both how the electronic properties of the substituent affect reactivity and explain directive effects. A complete exercise can be found at http://www.uccs.edu/~amschoff/chemexercise.html.

Variation: This exercise can be done with other types of reactions besides electrophilic aromatic substitution. For example, with slight modification, the closely related aromatic nucleophilic substitutions can be studied. Free radical substitutions at benzylic carbons can be analyzed in similar fashion.

WHO'S ON WELFARE?

GUEST AUTHOR: Tom Carskadon, Mississippi State University
DISCIPLINE: any academic discipline; also First-Year Experience courses

GOALS: When you get the feeling that your students are not putting a full-time effort into their studies, and they seem to resent a college-level workload, use this exercise to help them to think about why they are in school and who is really paying for it. Straight-forward lectures on the need and obligation to work hard are likely to be received with polite indifference, at best. This exercise, however, sets a trap of the students' own making, and it gets them to condemn their own work habits before they even realize that they have done so. As a side benefit, it may take a small step toward reducing any aspersion they may hold toward people who need public assistance.

This is an especially good exercise for first-year students, who may have gotten through high school surprisingly well with infrequent but judicious amounts of "stopgap study-ing." This exercise can be used with upperclass students, too. Every discipline requires a consistent academic work ethic, so this exercise can be useful with students in any major or field.

GROUP SIZE: any size of class you may be teaching

TIME REQUIRED: 15 to 30 minutes

MATERIALS: no special materials are required, although slide and PowerPoint users might enjoy adding some photo-visuals, such as a group of "workers" standing around doing nothing while only a few people are actually working.

PHYSICAL SETTING: Any setting in which you ordinarily meet your class, lab, or group will work fine.

PROCESS: Begin by asking your students if they have heard about the new welfare proposal. They are likely to give you blank looks, although some will visibly bristle at the very "mention" of welfare. Be vague about where you heard it—you think maybe NPR or CNN or someplace. It was just a little filler story, but it sounded like an interesting experiment, and if it proved successful, it would be introduced on a wide scale. Tell the students you can't quite remember all the details, but the gist of it is this:

It is a 5-year program designed to wean away "hard core" individuals who have been on the welfare rolls for years. Recipients will be placed in regular jobs—hamburger joints, discount stores, etc.—and receive minimum wage, to be provided by the government. Participating employers will simply be asked to take the workers; there will be no cost to the employers. This will give employers incentive to allow even inexperienced, unmotivated persons to work in their businesses. The employers do not choose the workers; they take whomever they are sent.

In year 1, employees will simply have to show up and observe; no work will be required, but they will be paid for full-time work. They may work if they want to, but the only requirement is that they be there and observe the other people working.

In year 2, employees must be there full time and actually work at least 10 hours a week (one-quarter time) in order to receive full-time pay. Again, they may work more, but they do not have to.

In year 3, employees must work 20 hours a week (one-half time) in order to receive full-time pay. For the other half of the time, they can stand around and watch.

In year 4, employees must work 30 hours a week (three-quarters time) for full-time pay, and they must at least observe the other workers—or help them out if they feel like it—for the other 10 hours a week.

In year 5, employees will have to work 40 hours a week (full time), just like any other worker, in order to get full-time pay.

After five years, the program is over, and participants should be used to working and ready to go out on their own and find regular, full-time positions in the job market.

Now, ask for student reactions to this plan. Some students will take the program at face value, and try to find some good in it. (After all, it is better than having people on welfare forever, etc.) Some will say the basic premise is good, but five years is way too long. Most students will hotly protest the whole program, appalled that people can be allowed to get full-time pay without full-time work; regular employees not in this unfair welfare program are working for their pay. Expect a number of venomous comments about lazy people on welfare ripping off the system, etc.

After this discussion goes on awhile, admit that there is no such program—you made the whole thing up—but you did want to see how the students would react to the idea. Ask them why they think you presented it to them. Odds are, they still won't get it!

Now shift the topic and ask how expensive college is compared to welfare. What do the students figure their college education is going to cost? Then point out the difference between public and private education. In nice round figures, a college education at a good state college or university will cost at least $30,000. Yet at a good private college or university, costs can easily go upwards of $120,000.

How can that be? Are the people running the private institutions stupid, or spendthrifts? Do the people running state colleges and universities know something the private schools do not? Of course, the difference is in public, taxpayer support of state colleges and institutions. The students will usually bring this up fairly quickly, yet most of them still will not have recognized the trap you have set.

Using the above figures, we would have to say that indirectly, the average student at a state school is getting at least $22,500 in benefits each year—quite possibly more than the median salary of citizens employed at full-time jobs in your state. Assuming a 15-week semester, that equals about $750 per week in "welfare" for each student.

Should taxpayers expect "full-time" work from students? Are students who take the money but "just watch," or students who only work on their studies part of the time, if and when they feel like it, any better than the welfare recipients in the above story? This simple exercise gets students thinking. . . .

(By the way, when students tell me "Dr. C., I pay your salary," I always respond with "Wrong! You are paying very little in taxes right now, but let me tell you: 'I' pay 'your' tuition!")

VARIATION: We developed this exercise at a comprehensive state university. If you teach in a private institution, you can easily adapt the principle by pointing out, quite truthfully, that even the prodigious sums that students pay in tuition at private colleges and universities cover only a fraction of the actual cost of their education. The rest comes from gifts and endowments, government grants and contracts, etc. And don't forget how many students have federally funded scholarships, guaranteed student loans, private scholarships, etc. Is it okay to accept this "welfare" from taxpayers, alumni, and donors, and not work full time in return? No way!

So, What's the Story?

Guest Author: Maryanne Wanca-Thibault, University of Colorado at Colorado Springs

Discipline: Communication

Goals: to encourage self-disclosure and raise awareness about sensitive or controversial issues common to the group and to provide new students a safe environment to get acquainted and learn about an issue through the eyes of their peers

This activity allows students to engage in discussions about topics or issues without labeling them as their own experiences. Instructors may choose to use this exercise as an icebreaker or as a teaching tool with a group at any point in the semester.

Group size: 10–15 Students

Time required: about 25 to 35 minutes. All students are asked to participate in the storytelling process at least one time.

Materials: none

Physical setting: The activity works best in a setting where the group can sit together and face each other.

Process: The instructor begins the storytelling process around the selected topic (e.g., "There once was a freshman who was beginning college at the University of Colorado. S/he had just checked into the dorm and as s/he looked out the window s/he began thinking about what the first couple of weeks would be like at this new place. The first thing that came to mind was..."). Each student then adds something to build on the story. Depending on the issue, the students, and the direction the story takes, the instructor may continue for more than one round. Once the story comes to a conclusion the instructor should spend time debriefing students about the activity.

Some suggested questions might include:
- What do we know about the topic/issue that we didn't know before?
- Were the students surprised by the responses of their peers?
- How does the story relate to the principles and goals the instructor has in mind?
- Are there other issues that weren't addressed in the story that could add to an understanding of the principles/concepts?

Variation: While this activity is useful at the start of the semester, it can be used at any point to generate discussion with the group (e.g., discussion might include sensitive topics such as cheating, stress, drugs, sexual relationships). The goal is to raise awareness of the common concerns and experiences that students have but might not otherwise share.

Orchestrating Peer-Response Sessions

Guest Author: Harriet Napierkowski, University of Colorado at Colorado Springs

Discipline: Composition and Rhetoric

Goals: Peer-response groups, in which students work in small groups reading and responding to one another's papers-in-progress, have been hailed as an innovation in writing instruction despite the fact that they have a long history in American pragmatism. Grounded in social constructivist theory, research on peer-response groups has indicated several benefits, among them, helping students give constructive feedback to one another through a reciprocal and participatory model of writing. Working in peer-response groups also increases motivation to perform, leads to improved interpersonal relations among its members, and improves self-esteem, allowing students to demonstrate individual strengths, build self-confidence, and take risks.

In regard to audience, peer response helps overcome what Piaget has termed egocentrism, a person's failure to perceive other people's perspectives. Peer response helps writers build an increased consideration for their readers. Through dialogue, students discover something about their use of language and can clarify their messages by rethinking, reshaping, and rewriting. As students engage in peer review of papers, they begin to be more aware of varieties in content, style, flavor, and diction. While some first-year composition students have already developed a sophisticated awareness of audience in their discourse, this tends to be the exception rather than the rule, and an immersion in peer-response pedagogy can help students increase such awareness.

Vygotsky's perspective on learning lends further support for the use of peer-response groups during the writing process in the construction and negotiation of meaning. In Vygotskian terms, learning is not an individual but rather a social activity, mediated by social interaction. Thus, peer-response groups can facilitate writing development by allowing students to construct meaning in the context of social interaction, allowing students to move beyond their level of functioning, what Vygotsky calls the "zone of proximal development." And teachers' use of peer-response groups signals their respect for students' knowledge-building capabilities.

Group size: 16–24 students, 4 students to each group (strategy can also work with smaller or larger groups, however).

Time required: 15–20 minutes per author in each group for a total of about 75 minutes.

Materials: Students bring four photocopies of their papers (encourage typed, penultimate drafts) with them to class. They also need pens or pencils for taking notes and a writing surface (clipboard or desk area).

Physical setting: Movable seating is preferable. Students work in clusters of four, each group moving their chairs into a circular configuration.

Process:
1. Divide the class into groups of four.
2. Advise the students about the protocol and purpose of the peer-response session.
   a. Students should take notes on a sheet of paper divided into three columns headed "plus," "minus," and "questions." They should jot down positive responses in the plus column, concerns in the minus column, and puzzlements in the questions column.
   b. Student should focus on ideas, clarity of purpose, and sufficiency of support/reasoning. Discourage students from focusing on grammar and mechanics (which is what they will otherwise tend to do). Editing should be addressed in a separate follow-up session.
   c. Students should back up comments with specific examples from the paper.
3. Students distribute their papers to their group members, keeping a copy for themselves as well.
4. In round-robin fashion, the first student's paper is read and then discussed. The student to the left of the student-author acts as facilitator, so that during the course of the session, each student acts as a facilitator for discussing someone's paper. Each student, in turn, states his/her response to the paper—what worked, what didn't, and what may have been confusing or unclear.
5. The author listens and takes notes during this process, without trying to defend the paper.
6. After the session, each student considers the feedback given and revises the paper for submission to the instructor the following class session.
7. Students earn points for participating in the peer-response session.

Variation:
1. Students read the papers out loud rather than silently.
2. Students take copies of the group's papers home, read and respond to them out of class, and prepare for small group discussion the following class period.
3. If time is short, students work in groups of three.
4. Students work in pairs, and each pair exchanges papers with another pair. Each pair of students responds to another pair's papers collaboratively.
5. For a more directive, guided approach, the instructor gives the students a set of prompts or a checklist to follow.

Film Evaluation Worksheet

Guest Author: Robert von Dassanowsky, University of Colorado at Colorado Springs
Discipline: Film and Media Studies; Cultural Studies

Goals: This exercise is intended to deconstruct short sequences or scenes from narrative films in order to underscore the choices of the filmmaker(s) and the building blocks of the message(s) conveyed to the audience through the various channels of information (sound, lighting, editing, costume, set, etc.). The hands-on opportunity for students of introductory level film/ media/cultural studies to examine a film of their choice through a sample dissection of its elements can demonstrate the technological complexity and artistry of filmmaking—as well as its sociopolitical value. The worksheet's systematic structure, individualization, and goal orientation also serves to empower the student who fears a lack of knowledge in film or visual arts: the analysis proves to be user-friendly, enlightening, and even fun. Often, introductory film and media study students are intimidated by technical and stylistic jargon. A lecture on the information embedded in a filmmaker's *mise-en-scene* can be needlessly complicated and dull. This self-starting activity, based in a film familiar to the student, will produce an informative process and result, regardless of the cinematic background of the student. It is based on the general pattern of analysis found in most introductory film studies texts and can be adapted to suit specific or localized examinations that may utilize film, such as sociopolitical, cultural, historical, literary, and gender studies.

Group size: no limit. This exercise is done individually and then can be discussed in a group.

Time required: Varies. The viewing or re-viewing of the entire film is required. The time for choice of segment (no longer than a five-minute scene or sequence) and repeated viewing for data depends on the student. Most students can complete this assignment in a few days.

Materials: Video or DVD of a narrative film; pen, worksheet

Physical setting: indoor space where a film can be viewed and paused

Process: The film evaluation worksheet can be adapted to suit different goals in the study of film, media, or cultural information conveyed by the media. Basic format follows.

Film Evaluation Worksheet

Select an approximate five-minute sequence from a film of your choice. Respond to the questions in a clear, concise manner. Respond to "Suggests?" by considering what effect the filmmakers intended with this choice.

I. Narration

    A. Describe the events which transpire in the plot during the selected sequence.
    B. How does this selected sequence fit into the overall film plot?
    C. Are there individual scenes in your segment? If so, separate them by location, time, characters.

II. Composition:

    A. Is the frame open or closed? Suggests?
    B. Is the space interior/exterior; cluttered/empty? Suggests?
    C. Are the sets studio/location? Suggests?
    D. Do certain props stand out? Do they seem symbolic? Suggests?
    E. Artistic design—Is the set realistic or stylized? Is it historical, contemporary, or does it evoke a particular artistic style? Suggests?
    F. View of the characters—Where are they in relation to each other and the set? Are they isolated/off-center/centered/background/foreground/obscured by or linked to objects? Suggests?
    G. Movement of characters—Where and how do they move within the sequence? Do characters acknowledge each other or not? Suggests?

III. Photography

    A. Shot—extreme long shot/long shot/medium shot/close-up/extreme close-up? Suggests?
    B. Lens—normal, wide-angle, fisheye, telephoto, distorting? Suggests?
    C. Focus—deep/soft/sharp (who and what is in/out of focus)? Suggests?
    D. Angle—high/low/eye-level/bird's-eye/worm's-eye, oblique? Suggests?
    E. Type of Shot—establishing/point of view/reaction/insert/flashback? Suggests?
    F. Movement—How and where does the camera move? From above/below/in/out/circular/zoom/fast/slow/handheld camera/mounted on vehicle? Suggests?
    G. Lighting—realistic/high key/low key/high contrast/outdoor or natural/lighting effects? Suggests?
    H. Color—black and white/sepia/color/mixed? Specific color scheme? Strong/faded colors? Warm/cool colors? Symbolic use of color or black and white in sets, props, costumes? Color effects? Suggests?
    I. Special effects—slow motion, filters, fast, reverse motion, odd points of view, digitally enhanced or generated views and/or images? Suggests?

IV. Sound

    A. Dialogue—actual dialogue/silence? Language quality or style (dialect or accent linked to period, culture, class, nationality, education, other films or texts)? Suggests?

    B. Music—on or off screen? Classical/popular/rock/jazz, etc.? As theme of a character or action? Subtle/dominant/irritating? Suggests?

    C. Voiceover or Narration—when/why/who? Reliable or unreliable? Suggests?

    D. Sound effects—natural/artificial? Part of action or outside of the reality of the film? Suggests?

V. Editing

    A. What preceded and what follows your segment? Suggests?

    B. Transition techniques—cut/fade in or out/dissolve/wipe jump cut? Suggests?

    C. Length of the shots—are some noticeably longer or shorter than others? Suggests?

    D. Pace and Rhythm—flowing/disjointed/abrupt/long panning shots/fast cuts? Do sequences differ in feel due to editing pace? Suggests?

VI. Additional Observations

    A. Acting—natural/stylized/mixed? Signifies?

    B. Costume design—symbolic/cultural signifier/(in-)accurately historical/stylized/linked to character or to setting? Suggests?

    C. Motifs—reoccurring visual concepts/actions/settings/props/sounds/music/gestures? Suggests?

    D. Cultural and Social coding—where/when? Strong or weak sense of time and place? Suggests?

VII. Total Evaluation

Utilizing the information above and in then re-viewing the entire film:

Does the film follow your expectations or what you consider cinematic convention or does it reject/subvert/question these?

Does the film address social/political/religious/cultural/historical issues? Does it address them in a controversial manner? Does it avoid issues?

Does the film manipulate the audience into identifying with certain characters or actions?

Does the film recognize the audience (e.g., characters looking into the camera; dialogue aimed directly at audience) or itself as a film?

Does the film offer particular originality, complexity, intensity, fantasy?

Given the above examination, how does the film succeed or not succeed (in its era) in bringing its information and point of view to the audience?

Variation: This exercise can be adapted to focus on specific aspects of media/cultural studies such as:

- Gender roles (in the given era).
- Approaches used in adaptation of literature to visual medium.
- Aspects of sociology and psychology (of the characters and their motivations in the given time and place of the film's production).
- Historical reception and propaganda (comparing different films on same or similar subjects from different eras or national cinemas).
- Understanding the implementation of specific artistic styles and movements in costume, furniture, and decorative design.
- Styles and manipulative use of music in the visual media.
- Cultural aspects and differences (similar topics presented by different national cinemas).

INTRODUCTION TO MAP AND COMPASS

GUEST AUTHOR: Thomas P. Huber, University of Colorado at Colorado Springs

DISCIPLINE: Geography

GOALS: This activity is a field experience that introduces students to the principles of using a topographic map and compass to navigate. The skills learned in the class are academically challenging and, at the same time, very useful to students who hike, ski, boat, or bicycle. The stated goals of the class are to develop topographic map-reading and compass skills that give students the self-confidence they need to use the learned techniques after the class is over. The experience also subtly encourages a renewed (or newly found) respect for the natural environment. This happens because the students are immersed in the outdoors for long periods during the course and cannot help but see the inherent beauty of the natural world. Secondary goals for the experience include the practical application of relatively simple mathematics, contact with the principles and materials of the earth sciences, an emphasis on accurate and careful application of knowledge, and social skills engendered by working in groups.

Some of the course is conducted in a traditional classroom setting. Learning about map symbols, map scale, the parts of the compass, and other skills are accomplished through lecture and sample problems. But the real, long-term learning takes place outside at the site of the actual map use. When we get to the field each day, the students practice their newly learned skills in a real-world situation. They will actually use the map and compass to navigate courses set up by the instructor. These courses vary from simple ones that take 15 minutes to longer ones that may take 1½ to 2 hours to complete. For some students this is the first time that they have ever been "out" in nature without the family car surrounding them. This is an intense experience for many, and this intensity is one of the real motivators and stimuli for learning. There is also an honest feeling of camaraderie among the students because they are dealing with the apprehension of this unfamiliar task.

GROUP SIZE: For reasons of safety, I recommend no more than twenty students in the class. I often try to have a teaching assistant (TA) who has taken the class previously to help with organizing the students and setting up the map-reading courses as described below.

TIME REQUIRED: This is a very time-intensive class. It is usually taught over six full days, with five half-days devoted to the outdoor portion of the class. Usually, the class cannot be held on campus, because there is no appropriate open area for the fieldwork. This means that students must drive themselves to the field site each day, or that the campus must provide transportation.

MATERIALS: The activity requires good topographic maps of your field site. Some communities have orienteering clubs that have produced very high-quality maps for just this kind of activity. In most cases you will be able to get U.S. Geological Survey maps at a scale of 1:24000 or better. The students will also need a good quality compass, which can be purchased at outdoor shops for under $20. Hiking boots/walking shoes, appropriate clothing, water, sunscreen, and snack food is also suggested.

PHYSICAL SETTING: Fortunately, I have several large, undeveloped city parks that are close to our campus to go to for my fieldwork. One of these has high-quality orienteering maps produced for it, which makes the site perfect. In lieu of this ideal situation, regional or state parks, National Forests, or other public open places could be used. If you use private land, you must make sure you have been granted the appropriate permissions. But with a little creativity, field exercises can even be done in urban areas. Once I ran one of these courses for elementary school students and just used a hand-drawn map and the schoolyard; the students loved it!

PROCESS: The first day outside, I show the students the map symbols and what those symbols represent on the ground. I also take all of the students on a walking tour of the area using the map. I stop often to orient them, and I show how the land surface matches what is on the map. This first orientation is critical for making the students comfortable about being "let loose" on their own. The critical core of the fieldwork, however, is the running (usually very slow walking in reality) of the orienteering course that I, or the TA, have set up. The first day, this course is very short, and the students do it in groups of four or five. Each day the course gets longer and more complicated as the students' skill and confidence increase. I also insist that the groups get progressively smaller. By the last day, each student will be doing the course by her or himself. The courses consist of markers set in various locations that vary each day. These locations are marked on a master map that the students copy onto their own maps. Then they must go find the markers in sequential order and return to the starting point. Each marker has a unique identifier that the students must record to show that they have, in fact, found it. It is critical that you keep track of when each student leaves the start line and when she or he returns—no excuses for losing a student!

VARIATION: There are many, many variations to this course. I have taken students to remote mountain cabins in the winter where we stayed for a week and did the map courses on cross-country skis. You can teach map and compass skills on mountain bikes, canoes, or even in cars (rallies). It is great fun for any age student. I have taught elementary school, middle school and high school students, and they all seem to love it!

CULTURAL ICONS

AUTHOR: Steve Staley, Colorado Technical University

DISCIPLINE: Humanities—"World Cultures and Values"

GOALS: In the first hour of your first class meeting, this exercise will help you:
1. take the roll creatively
2. facilitate students learning each other's backgrounds and interests
3. begin the process of inductively defining "culture"
4. realize the breadth and variation in cultural understanding students bring and by implication, they sense their limitations and challenges as well
5. prepare students to learn in a more disciplined and inclusive fashion the nature of human cultures and values

GROUP SIZE: almost any size class, from twelve to forty or more

TIME REQUIRED: about five minutes of reflecting and writing, followed by ten minutes of student interaction and a half hour (or more) of introductions and discussion. Depending on the size of your class, this could take from 45 minutes to over an hour.

MATERIALS: the "Cultural Icon" sheet that follows, although this is not necessary to do the exericse

PHYSICAL SETTING: a normal classroom, with the ability for students to get up and move around during the exercise.

PROCESS: On the first day of History 245, "Global Cultures and Values," I begin the class by passing out a sheet of paper entitled "Cultural Icons." I ask each student to think of someone from either the past or present who is a "cultural icon," and write that person's name at the top of the sheet. Then the student is to think of three clues to the identity of this famous person. The first clue should be somewhat difficult, the second more easily guessed, and the third should give the answer away.

When students ask, "What do you mean by 'cultural icon'?" (and they always will), I tell them to do their best to imagine what that term might mean, and select someone who fits their definition. Rather than define the term for them, I ask them to use their own working definition for the time being.

When students have filled out their sheets, I ask them to get up from their seats, move around the room, and trade clues with each other, one on one. Each student should try to guess another student's "cultural icon" based on the clues that student reads aloud, while other students are similarly engaged around the classroom. If a student guesses the icon correctly after the first clue, the student gets to initial clue number one on the icon sheet—or clue two or three, if guessed then. Part of the game is to see how many times each student can earn the right to scribble her or his initials in the three clue columns. Let them know you'll be playing, too—and play with enthusiasm in a friendly, accessible fashion.

You may occasionally have to prompt students to move about in order to find new subjects. But after about ten minutes of high-energy interaction, ask the class to return to their seats. Now it's time to take the roll, and I do so by telling students I'm NOT going to go down the class roster alphabetically. Rather, I'm going to ask them to tell us their names, academic majors, one or more unusual places they've lived or traveled, and finally who they picked as their "cultural icon"—and most importantly, why! Then I ask, "Who'd like to start?"

As the first student raises her or his hand, I encourage the rest of the class to write down names and important bits of information as they listen. When the initial student names her "cultural icon" and tells why she picked that person, comment on why that choice was particularly apt, why that person is indeed an "icon" and represents a given culture, people, movement, or set of values—and ask for additional comments from the class. Then ask "Who's next?" and continue until everyone has had a chance.

The range of "cultural icons" your students will pick will most likely surprise and gratify you. My students have come up with such representative figures as Martin Luther King Jr. (one of the most popular), Abraham Lincoln, Mother Theresa, Joseph Stalin, Fidel Castro, Mahatma Gandhi, William Shakespeare, and even Genghis Khan! In the ensuing short explanations and discussions of why and how each is a "cultural icon," you guide the class into an understanding not only of the nature of an "icon" but also of the breadth and variation of such icons and the cultures and values they represent.

Occasionally a student will come up with a name you (and the rest of the class) haven't heard of. Make the best of the situation by emphasizing the strengths of the student's explanation, let them know you've learned something important, and move on to the next student.

You might end by giving them dictionary (or text) definitions of "culture" and "icon," but however you capitalize on this exercise, your students will begin the course actively stimulated to want more.

VARIATION: With a little imagination, this exercise could be varied to fit a variety of different subject matters—U.S. History, Western Civilization, Sociology, Literature, etc.

CULTURAL ICONS: Who Am I?

The cultural icon whose identity I'm assuming is _____.

Clue #1:

Clue #2:

Clue #3:

Initials of those who guess correctly after:

Clue #1_____   Clue #2_____   Clue #3_____

"Dear Desdemona..."

Guest Author: Steve Staley, Colorado Technical University

Discipline: Literature

Goals: This activity focuses on character analysis, including a character's motivation, insight, and planning based on an understanding of human psychology and interaction. It also exercises both oral and written communication skills. The creative nature of the assignment should also make it impossible for a student to locate and download a paper from the Internet—currently an all-too-common possibility.

Group size: any size class, from 12 to approximately 40

Time required: approximately 40 minutes

Materials: none

Physical setting: normal classroom

Process: This activity requires students to write a letter of warning to a fictional character in a crisis situation. The example used here is the situation of Desdemona in Shakespeare's *Othello*.

Once your students have read the play, begin your discussion of the basics of character and plot. As the discussion comes around to Desdemona, but before discussing in any depth her strengths, weaknesses, and characteristics, tell your students you'd like them to try an exercise designed to help them see her situation as more realistic, more personal, and more consequential.

Describe this situation to your students: You're living at the time of the story, and you're acquainted with Desdemona and the other major characters in the play. You've observed what happens as Iago begins to work on Othello's imagination, planting the seeds of jealousy in suggesting that there just may be something happening between Desdemona and Cassio. If you were to warn Desdemona at this juncture, what would you say? What would you deliberately avoid saying? What might be the consequences of your intervention?

Task 1: Ask your students to form two-person teams. Each team should take ten minutes to pre-write a letter to Desdemona—what should the letter say, in what tone, with what facts or warnings or advice?

It's up to each team to decide just how they will handle the situation—don't elaborate upon or restrict their concept of the task. Just be certain to tell them exactly at what point in the play their letter is being written, sent, and read by Desdemona. I suggest right after Act III, scene III, when Iago has acquired Desdemona's handkerchief and just before Othello asks Desdemona where it is.

Task 2: When their time is up, tell them to take home with them their notes on the letter, and that for the next class meeting you'd like each *individual* to turn in an actual letter based on their team decision.

Task 3: During this next session you may ask volunteers to read from their letters. Or better yet, divide the class into groups of three or four, ensuring that the two-person team members from the prior class are in different groups. Ask the groups to read their letters aloud, discuss the wisdom and effectiveness of the various letters, and when the class is reassembled, ask each group to report on some of the more "interesting" or effective letters they reviewed.

Use the ensuing discussion to help your students gain deeper insights into the character of Desdemona, the challenges she faces, and the chances that she may or may not be able to change the outcome of the story—all in light of Othello's and Iago's most likely reactions to their "interference."

Variations: This exercise may be varied in a number of ways. You may allow class members to choose individually which characters they'd like to write to. Perhaps one would actually write to Othello, or to Cassio. The more determined or adventurous might even write to Iago! And of course you might use this exercise in any other drama, novel, or short story in which a character faces a threat or challenge worth warning about.

Closing Exercises

Part II of *50 Ways to Leave Your Lectern* began with the notion that one of the most critical aspects of your first-year course is "building" the group, forming "one" from "many." Ending the course, however, saying goodbye, and bringing closure are also important, especially in the long run. After all, what happens afterward—in terms of students integrating what they have learned into a larger body of knowledge and broader academic reality—is the real test of learning, no matter how enjoyable the experience has been.

Activities in this section focus on helping you:

- **Return to the goals you outlined in the beginning.**

- **Help students feel they have contributed.**

- **Provide opportunities to think about integration.**

- **Encourage continuing connections between students.**

- **Communicate your willingness to remain in a support role.**

- **End on a high note.**

Award Ceremony

Goals: to help students remember each other and feel valued for their contributions

Group size: any size group

Time required: 2–4 minutes per student

Materials: an award certificate (template on the following page) and an inexpensive, humorous gift for each student

Physical setting: normal classroom

Process: This exercise is a great deal of fun and makes each student feel "honored" for some contribution she or he has made to the group. The gifts should be inexpensive "trinkets" and caricature the individual. For example, in my course, one student wrote a paper on teenage marriage, and she was awarded the Freshman Seminar "Let Them Eat Cake" Award of a Duncan Hines (wedding?) cake mix. Another student from California, who was adjusting to the Colorado snow, received a pair of mittens and the "California Dreamin'" Award.

Variation: Create your own template, using your school's logo, etc., or purchase ready-made "authentic-looking" certificates from a stationery store. Adjust the course title on the certificate to match the course in which you're giving awards.

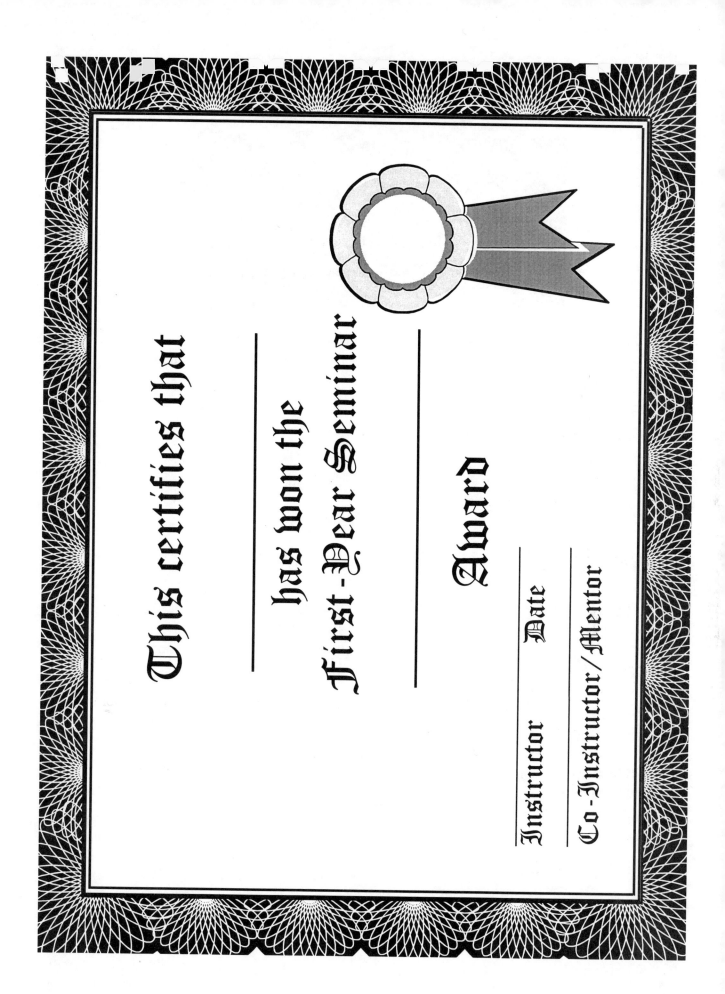

This certifies that

_____

has won the

First-Year Seminar

Award

_____

Instructor   Date

Co-Instructor/Mentor

177

Goals: to help the group say goodbye and take a memento of the class with them

Group size: any size group

Time required: 20–30 minutes

Materials: a snapshot of the group for each participant

Physical setting: normal class/training room

Process: Take a photo of the group and distribute a reprint or color copy to each member during the last group meeting (or scan in the photo, enlarge it, and make color copies). Allow participants to circulate and sign the back of each other's photos. (Naturally, larger photos are easier to write on.) Individuals may make comments such as

- "This picture would be incomplete without you because…"
- "You're unforgettable because…"
- "At first I thought you were _____, but…"
- "Your contribution to our group was…"
- "What I'll remember about you most is…"

Variation: Use a digital camera and put the photos on the class website (if your school allows).

Learning Collage

Goals: to help students assess their own learning and provide feedback

Group Size: any size class

Time required: 15–45 minutes

Materials: one sticky note per participant

Physical Setting: normal classroom

Process: Give participants sticky notes and ask them to write the most important point, concept, fact, etc. learned during the course. Ask them to stick their notes to a large posterboard or sheet of newsprint displayed in a prominent place and to read and compare what they have learned with others' responses.

Variation: Rather than at the end of a course, this exercise may be done as a midpoint check. Or ask participants to identify one point they would like to learn that has not been covered yet.

A Letter for Later

Goals: to help students remember the lessons they have learned and keep commitments they have made

Group size: any size group

Time required: 20–30 minutes (or as an outside assignment)

Materials: paper and envelopes

Physical setting: normal classroom (or given as a homework assignment)

Process: Ask students to write themselves a letter which you will mail to them in a designated amount of time (six weeks, six months, at the end of the next term, etc.). To go along with the letter, they should self-address an envelope. In the letter, they should cover points such as the following:

- "My goals for the coming (weeks, month, term) are…"
- "I'll use the skills I've developed here by…"
- "In this class, I've learned that…"
- "In six weeks (six months, etc.), I predict that I'll…"

Variation: Ask students to write about their future goals to one another or to a friend or parent who can serve as a coach and provide support.

You Know What I Really Like About You?

Goals: to help students say goodbye and take positive memories from the course

Group size: any size group

Time required: 15–30 minutes

Materials: 1 sheet of posterboard, with two holes punched near the top and strung with ribbon, and a colored marker for each student

Physical setting: outside or in a room large enough for participants to circulate from one person to another

Process: Each student should write the following phrase at the top of his or her sheet of posterboard: "This Is What I Really Like About You…" After "putting on" their posterboards (to wear them on their backs), students should circulate around the room and sign each other's boards by finishing the statement with a specific characteristic they admired about that person during the course.

Variation: Additional unfinished statements may be created; however, statements should not be threatening or inadvertently allow the opportunity for negative comments.

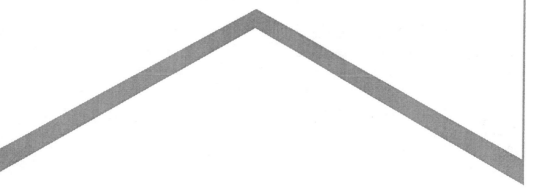

181

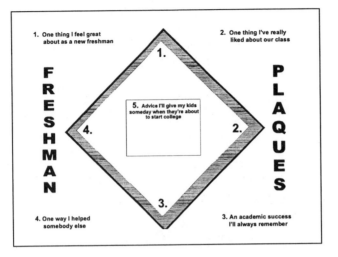

Goals: to help first-year students reflect on their new experiences in college, receive confirmation for their successes, and summarize the lessons they have learned

Group size: any size group may begin the exercise, but preliminary processing should occur in pairs or small groups before reconvening as a larger group

Time required: approximately 30 minutes to 1 hour

Materials: one plaque per student (reproduced on paper or cardstock using the following page), or you may provide the template and have students construct their own plaque on paper or newsprint

Physical setting: a classroom large enough for students to work on the floor (if using newsprint) and to discuss in pairs or small groups

Process: Ask each student to respond to the statements by writing or drawing a response in each corner of their plaque. You might expect responses such as the following:

1. One thing I feel great about as a new freshman: that my grades were better than I expected, that I worked out the problems with my roommate, that I made a lot of friends, etc.
2. One thing I've really liked about our class: I've felt comfortable and accepted, that we talked about how to succeed and it worked, that we were involved learners, etc.
3. An academic success I'll always remember: getting an A in composition, that I can speak French much better than in high school, etc.
4. One way I helped somebody else: I helped my best friend tough it out in Philosophy, that I led a study team in Algebra, etc.
5. Advice I'll give my kids: College is hard work but fun; you should use high school to get ready for college and not just to have a good time; you should start saving

money early to pay for college; college is a place to meet people who are different from you in many ways and to learn from them, etc.

After they have filled in their plaques, ask students to discuss them in pairs or small groups (to lower any perceived threat of speaking out in a large group since responses are personal), followed by a general discussion in the group as a whole.

Variation: Vary the questions to suit your purposes, based on the particular characteristics of your course or the group of students you are working with. You may also include "lessons learned" with questions such as "One thing I didn't know as well as I thought I did," "One thing I'd like a second chance at," or "One important thing I've learned."

Based on "Secret Support" in Solem, L. & Pike, B. (1997). *50 creative training closers*.
San Francisco: Jossey-Bass, 84–85.

Goals: to help first-year students reconnect after the course is over and receive support in meeting goals they have set

Group size: any size group

Time required: approximately 15 minutes to set up, completed later outside of class

Materials: one index card per student

Physical setting: any size classroom

Process: Hand out index cards at the end of the course, and ask each student to provide the following information:

1. Name
2. Email address
3. Phone number
4. A goal he or she will set for the following term
5. How he or she would like to be contacted in _____ (set a time: one month, two months, around midterms)
6. What he or she would like in the way of support from the classmate who contacts him or her

Collect the completed cards, shuffle them, and redistribute one to each student, making sure no student receives his or her own card back.

Variation: Vary the questions to suit your purposes, based on the particular characteristics of your course or the group of students you are working with.

GROUP MURAL

Based on "Group Mural" in Eitington, J. E. (1996).
The winning trainer (3rd edition). Houston: Gulf Publishing, 57.

Goals: to help a student group reflect on its history, summarize the course, and say goodbye

Group size: a small class of 10–15 students works best

Time required: exercise may last up to one hour

Materials: give students numerous markers to work with and a long roll of newsprint (or several newsprint sheets taped together) to fill an entire wall or wrap around the room

Physical setting: a normal classroom setting (or outside on a sidewalk)

Process: Ask the group to reflect on its history since the course began and create a pictorial record for "posterity," depicting the highs and lows of the course, the personalities of class members, the various assignments, what they've learned, their feelings about college now, etc.

Variation: Take a group photo of the class in front of the mural when it's done and send an email copy to each student after the class is over as a "souvenir."

Suggested
Readings

ACT. (2002). *2001 ACT national and state scores*. Retrieved February 20, 2002, from http://www.act.org/news/data/01/tsum.html

Abel, D. (2000, 29 December). How much does college teach—and should we care? *The Boston Globe*. Retrieved July 26, 2001, from http://www.indiana.edu/nsse/articles/seattlepi_1229.htm

Amey, M. J. (1999). Faculty culture and college life: Reshaping incentives toward student outcomes. *New Directions for Teaching and Learning, 105*, 59–69.

Anchors, W. S., Robbins, M. A., & Gershman, E. S. (1989). The relationship between Jungian type and persistence to graduation among college students. *Journal of Psychological Type, 17*, 20–25.

Anderson, J. (2001, March). Tailoring assessment to student learning styles. *AAHE Bulletin*. Retrieved June 6, 2001, from http://www.aahe.org/bulletin/styles.htm

Anderson, R. S., & Speck B. W. (1998). Changing the way we grade student performance: Classroom assessment and the new learning paradigm. *New Directions for Teaching and Learning, 74*.

Angelo, T. A. (1991). Ten easy pieces: Assessing higher learning in four dimensions. *New Directions for Teaching and Learning, 46*, 17–31.

Angelo, T. A. (1993). A "Teacher's Dozen": Fourteen general, research-based principles for improving higher learning in our classrooms. *AAHE Bulletin*, 3–7, 13.

Angelo, T. A. (1999, May). Doing assessment as if learning matters most. *AAHE Bulletin*. Retrieved June 10, 2001 from http:www.aahe.org/Bulletin/angelomay99.htm

Angelo, T. A., & Cross, P. (1993). *Classroom assessment techniques: A handbook for college teachers* (2nd ed.). San Francisco: Jossey-Bass.

Astin, A. (1970). The methodology of research on college impact (I). *Sociology of Education, 43*, 223–254.

Astin, A. (1984). Student involvement: A developmental theory for higher education. *Journal of College Student Personnel, 25*, 297–308.

Astin, A. (1985). *Achieving educational excellence: A critical assessment of priorities and practices in higher education*. San Francisco: Jossey-Bass.

Astin, A. (1993). *What matters in college?* San Francisco: Jossey-Bass.

Astin, A., Banta, T. W., Cross, K. P., El-Khawas, E., Ewell, P. T., Hutching, P., et al. (2001). *Assessment forum: 9 principles of good practice for assessing student learning*. Retrieved June 5, 2001, from http://www.aahe.org/assessment/principl.htm

Auster, C. J., & MacRone, M. (1994). The classroom as a negotiated social setting: An empirical study of the effects of faculty members' behavior on students' participation. *Teaching Sociology, 22*, 289–300.

Azwell, T. S. (1995). Alternative assessment forms. In H. C. Foyle (Ed.). *Interactive learning in the higher education classroom: Cooperative, collaborative, and active learning strategies* (pp. 160–174). Washington D.C.: National Education Association.

Banta, T. W., Lund, J. P., Black, K. E., & Oblander, F. W. (1996). *Assessment in practice: Putting principles to work on college campuses*. San Francisco: Jossey-Bass.

Barefoot, B. (1998). *National survey of freshman seminar programming*. University of South Carolina: National Resource Center for the First-Year Experience and Students in Transition.

Barefoot, B., Warnock, C., Dickinson, M., Richardson, S., & Roberts, M. (1998). *Exploring the evidence: Reporting outcomes of first-year seminars*, Vol. II. Columbia, SC: National Resource Center for the First-Year Experience and Students in Transition.

Barr, R. B., & Tagg, J. (1995, November–December). From teaching to learning—a new paradigm for undergraduate education. *Change, 27*(6), 12–25.

Bartlett, T. (2002, February 1). Freshmen pay, mentally and physically, as they adjust to life in college. *The Chronicle of Higher Education,* pp.A35–38.

Belenky, M. B., Clinchy, B. M., Goldberger, N. R., & Tarule, J. M. (1986). *Women's ways of knowing*. New York: Basic Books.

Bess, J. L. (1997). *Teaching well and liking it*. Baltimore: Johns Hopkins University Press.

Bloom, B. S. (Ed.). (1956). *Taxonomy of educational objectives: The classification of educational goals*. New York: Longman.

Bloom, B. S. (1976). *Human characteristics and school learning*. New York: McGraw-Hill.

Boice, B. (1996). Classroom incivilities. *Research in Higher Education, 37*(4), 453–486.

Bonwell, C. C., & Eison. J. A. (1991). *Active learning: Creating excitement in the classroom*. ERIC Higher Education No. 1. Washington, DC: George Washington University, School of Education and Human Development.

Boyer Commission. (1998). Reinventing undergraduate education: A blueprint for America's research universities. Retrieved March 9, 2002, from http://naples.cc.sunysb.edu/Pres/boyer.nsf/

Braxton, J. M., Milem, J. F., Sullivan, A. S., & Shaw. (2000). The influence of active learning on the college student departure process. *Journal of Higher Education, 71*(5), 569-590.

Bringle, R. G., Games, R., & Malloy, E. A. (Eds). (1999). *Colleges and universities as citizens*. Needham Heights, MA: Allyn & Bacon.

Brookfield, S. D. (1990). *The skillful teacher*. San Francisco: Jossey-Bass.

Brookfield, S. D. (1995). *Becoming a critically reflective teacher*. San Francisco: Jossey-Bass.

Brookfield, S. D., & Preskill, S. (1999). *Discussion as a way of teaching*. San Francisco: Jossey-Bass.

Brown, S., Armstrong, S., & Thompson, G. (1998). *Motivating students*. London: Kogan Page.

Brown, S., & Race, P. (1996). *500 tips on assessment*. London: Kogan Page.

Caine, R. N., & Caine, G. (1991). *Making connections: Teaching and the human brain*. Alexandria, VA: Association for Supervision and Curriculum Development.

Cambridge, B. (2001, January). Assessing the real college experience. *AAHE Bulletin*. Retrieved June 6, 2001, from http://www.aahe.org/bulletin/real_college.htm

Campbell, W. E., & Smith, K. A. (Eds). (1997). *New paradigms for college teaching*. Edina, MN: Interaction Book Company.

Caprio, M. W., & Micikas, L. B. (1998). Getting there from here. *Journal of College Science Teaching, 27*(3), 217–221.

Chaffee, E. E. et al. (1997). *Assessing impact: Evidence and action*. Washington, DC: American Association for Higher Education.

Ewell, P. (1991). To capture the ineffable: New forms of assessment in higher education. In *Reprise 1991*. Washington, DC: American Association for Higher Education.

Ewell, P. (1997). Organizing for learning: A new initiative. *AAHE Bulletin*. Retrieved July 26, 2001 from http://www.psu.edu/dept/cac/ets/presentations/CatalystTexts/ewell.html

Ewell, P. (2000). *Grading student learning: Better luck next time*. Retrieved July 26, 2001, from http://measuringup2000.highereducation.org/PeterEwell.cfm

Eyler, J., & Giles, D. (1999). *Where's the learning in service-learning?* San Francisco: Jossey-Bass.

Eyler, J., Giles, D. E., Jr., & Schmiede, A. (1996). *A practitioner's guide to reflection in service-learning: Student voices and reflections*. Nashville, TN: Vanderbilt University.

Fassinger, P. A. (1997). Classes are groups: Thinking sociologically about teaching. *College Teaching, 45*(1), 22–225.

Faust, J. L., & Paulson, D. R. (1998). Active learning in the college classroom. *Journal on Excellence in College Teaching, 9*(2), 3–24.

Felder, R. (1993). What matters in college? *Chemical Engineering Education, 27*(4), 194–195.

Felder, R. M., & Brent, R. (1996). Navigating the bumpy road to student-centered instruction. *College Teaching, 44*, 43–47.

Fiorini, G. R., Miller, J., & Acusta, A. P. (1998). Developing activities for the mathematics classroom. *Mathematics and Computer Education, 32*(2), 174–187.

Fitts, C. T., & Swift, F. H. (1928). *The construction of orientation courses for college freshmen*. Berkeley, CA: University of California Publications in Education.

Foyle, H. C. (Ed.). (1995). *Interactive learning in the higher education classroom: Cooperative, collaborative, and active learning strategies*. Washington DC: National Education Association.

Gabelnick, F., MacGregor J., Matthews, R. S., and Smith, B. L. (1990). Learning communities: Building connections among students, faculty, and disciplines. *New Directions in Teaching and Learning, 41*.

Gardner, J. N. (1998, February). *Current trends in the first college year*. Faculty House Dinner Workshop conducted at the National Conference on the Freshman-Year Experience, Columbia, South Carolina.

Gardner, J. N., & Jewler, A. J. (2003). *Your college experience: Strategies for success* (5th ed.). Belmont, CA: Wadsworth.

Garko, M. G., Kough, C., Pignata, G., Kimmel, E. B., & Eison, J. (1995). Myths about student-faculty relationships: What do students really want? *Journal on Excellence in College Teaching, 5*(2), 51–65.

Gedeon, R. (1997). Enhancing a large lecture with active learning. *Research strategies, 15*(4), 301–309.

Gonzales, V., & Lopez, E. (2001, April). The age of incivility. *AAHE Bulletin*. Retrieved July 26, 2001, from http://www.aahe.org/bulletin/incivility.htm

Gordon, V. N, & Grites, T. J. (1984). The freshman seminar course: Helping students succeed. *Journal of College Student Personnel, 25*, 315–320.

Hatcher, J. A., & Bringle, R. G. (1997). Reflection: Bridging the gap between service and learning. *College Teaching, 45*(4), 153–158.

Hatfield, S. R. (Ed.) (1995). *The seven principles in action: Improving undergraduate education*. Bolton, MA: Anker Publishing Company.

Higbee, J. L., & Dwinell, P. L. (1995). Affect: How important is it? *Research and Teaching in Developmental Education, 12*(1), 71–74.

Higher Education Research Institute, UCLA. (no date). The American freshman: National norms. Retrieved March 10, 2002, from http://www.gseis.ucla.edu/heri/heri.html

Howard, J. R., Short, L. B., & Clark, S. M. (1996). Students' participation in the mixed-age college classroom. *Teaching Sociology, 24*, 8–24.

Howe, N., & Strauss, W. (2001). *Millennials rising: The next great generation*. New York: Vintage Books.

Hunter, M. S., & Skipper, T. (1999). *Solid foundations: Building success for first-year seminars through instructor training and development*. Columbia, SC: National Resource Center for The First-Year Experience and Students in Transition.

Hurtado, S., & Carter, D. F. (1997). Effects of college transition and perceptions of the campus racial climate on Latino college students' sense of belonging. *Sociology of Education, 70*, 324–345.

Iran-Nejad, A., & Chissom, B. S. (1992). Contributions of active and dynamic self-regulation to learning. *Innovative Higher Education, 17*(2), 125–136.

Jacob, S. W., & Eleser, C. B. (1997). Learner responsibility through "presence." *College Student Journal, 31*, 460–466.

Jensen, E., & Davidson, N. (1997). 12 step recovery program for lectureholics (based on 12 steps of Alcoholics Anonymous). *College Teaching, 45*, 102–103.

Johnson, D. W., Johnson, R. T., & Smith, K. A. (1992). *Cooperative learning: Increasing college faculty instructional productivity.* ASHE-ERIC Higher Education Report No. 4. Washington, DC: The George Washington University, School of Education and Human Development. (Eric Document Reproduction Service No. ED347871.) Retrieved on March 12, 2002, from http://ed.gov/databases.ERIC_Digests/ed347871.html

Junn, E. N. (1994). Experiential approaches to enhancing cultural awareness. In Diane F. Halpern (Ed.). *Changing college classrooms* (pp. 128–164). San Francisco: Jossey-Bass.

Kagan, S. (1992). *Cooperative learning.* San Juan Capistrano, CA: Resources for Teachers.

Kember, D., & Wong, A. (2000). Implications for evaluation from a study of students' perceptions of good and poor teaching. *Higher Education, 40*, 69–97.

King, A. (1993). From sage on the stage to guide on the side. *College Teaching, 41*(1), 30–35.

Kinzie, M. B, Hrabe, M. E., & Larsen, V. A. (1998). An instructional design case event: Exploring issues in professional practice. *Educational Technology Research and Development, 46*(1), 53–71.

Kirp, D. L. (1997, May/June). Those who can't: 27 ways of looking at a classroom. *Change*, 14.

Knight, P. (Ed.) (1995). *Assessment for learning in higher education.* London: Kogan Page.

Kolb, D. (1984). *Experiential learning: Experience as the source of learning and development.* New York: Prentice-Hall.

Kroehnrt, G. (1992). *100 training games*. New York: McGraw-Hill.

Kuh, I. (1999). How are we doing? Tracking the quality of the undergraduate experience, 1960s to the present. *The Review of Higher Education, 22*(2), 99–119.

Ku, G., & Vesper, N. (1997). A comparison of student experiences with good practices in undergraduate education between 1990 and 1994. *Review of Higher Education, 21*(1), 42–61.

uh, G., Pace, C., & Vesper, N. (1997). The development of process indicators to estimate student gains associated with good practices in undergraduate education. *Research in Higher Education, 38*(4), 435–454.

Leamnson, R.(1999). *Thinking about teaching and learning: Developing habits of learning with first year college and university students*. Sterling, VA: Stylus.

Leamnson, R. (2000). Learning as biological brain change. *Change, 32*(6), 34–40.

Leonard, W. H. (2000). How do college students best learn science? *Journal of College Science Teaching, 29*(6), 385–388.

Levine, A., & Cureton, J. S. (1998, May/June). Collegiate life: An obituary. *Change,* 14–17, 51.

Lindquist, T. M. (1997). An experimental test of cooperative learning with faculty members as subjects. *Journal of Education for Business, 72*(3), 157–163.

Livengood, J. M. (1992). Students' motivational goals and beliefs about effort and ability as they relate to college academic success. *Research in Higher Education, 33*(2), 247–261.

Lord, T. R. (1999). Are we cultivating "Couch Potatoes" in our college science lectures? *Journal of College Science Teaching, 29*(1), 59–62.

Lowery, J. W. (2001, July–August). The millennials come to campus. *About Campus*, pp 6–12.

Lowman, J. (1990). Promoting motivation and learning. *College Teaching, 38*(4), 136–139.

Lucas, A. F. (1990). Using psychological models to understand student motivation. In M. D. Svinicki (Ed.). *The changing face of college teaching. New Directions for Teaching and Learning, 42*. San Francisco: Jossey-Bass.

MacKinnon, M. M. (1999). CORE elements of student motivation in problem-based learning. *New Directions for Teaching and Learning, 78*, 49–58.

Marbach-Ad, G., Seal, O., & Sokolove, P. (2001). Student attitudes and recommendations on active learning. *Journal of College Science Teaching, 30*(7), 434–438.

Marchese, T. (1998, March/April). Disengaged students. *Change*, 4.

Marchese, T. J. (2001). The new conversations about learning: Insights from neuroscience and anthropology, cognitive science and work-place studies. *Assessing Impact: Evidence and Action*, 79-95. Retrieved January 11, 2001, from http://www.aahe.org/pubs/TM-essay.htm

McCarthy, J. P., & Anderson, L. (2000). Active learning techniques versus traditional teaching styles: Two experiments from history and political science. *Innovative Higher Education 24*(4), 279–294.

McGrath, E. (2001, September 10). Welcome, freshmen! *Time Magazine*, 64, 68, 71, 73–74.

McKeachie, W. J. (1986). *Teaching tips: A guidebook for the beginning college teacher* (8th ed.). Lexington, MA: D. C. Heath.

McKeachie, W. J., & Hofer, B. (2002). *Teaching tips: Strategies, research, and theory for college and university teachers*. (11th ed.). Boston: Houghton Mifflin.

McNeal, A. P. (1998). Death of the talking heads: Participatory workshops for curricular reform. *College Teaching, 46*(3), 90–92.

Media use in America. (2000). *Issue briefs: Media use in America*. Retrieved March 10, 2002, from http://www.mediascope.org/pubs/ibriefs/mua.htm

Menges, R. J. (1988). Research on teaching and learning: The relevant and the redundant. *Review of Higher Education, 11*, 259–268.

Meyers, C., & Jones, T. B. (1993). *Promoting active learning: Strategies for the college classroom*. San Francisco: Jossey-Bass.

Millis, B. J., & Cottell, P. G., Jr. (1998). *Cooperative learning for higher education faculty*. Phoenix, AZ: Oryx Press.

Montgomery, K., Brown, S., & Deery, C. (1997). Simulations: Using experiential learning to add relevancy and meaning to introductory courses. *Innovative Higher Education, 21*(3), 217–229.

Moore, R. L. (1998). Teaching introductory economics with a collaborative learning lab component. *The Journal of Economic Education, 29*(4), 321–329.

Myers, L. L. (1988). Teachers as models of active learning. *College Teaching, 36,* 43–45.

National Center for Postsecondary Improvement. (1999). Revolution or evolution? Gauging the impact of institutional student-assessment strategies. *Change, 31*(5), 53–57.

Newman, J. H. C. (1959). *The idea of a university.* Garden City, NJ: Image Books.

Newstrom, J., & Scannell, E. (1996). *The big book of business games.* New York: McGraw-Hill.

Newstrom, J., & Scannell, E. (1998). *The big book of team building games.* New York: McGraw-Hill.

Newton, F. B. (2000, November–December). The new student. *About Campus,* 8–15.

Nilson, L. B. (1998). *Teaching at its best: A research-based resource for college instructors.* Bolton, MA: Anker

Nora, A., Cabrera, A., Hagedorn, L. S., & Pascarella, E. T. (1996). Differential impacts of academic and social experiences on college-related behavioral outcomes versus different ethnic and gender groups at four-year institutions. *Research in Higher Education, 37,* 427–452.

Nunn, C. E. (1996). Discussion in the college classroom: Triangulating observational and survey results. *Journal of Higher Education, 67*(3), 244–266.

Olivo, J. J., Cecco, S. A., & Kieser, A. L. (2001). Getting your students involved on day one. *Business Education Forum, 55*(3), 52–55.

Orridge, M. (1996). *75 ways to liven up your training: A collection of energizing activities.* Hampshire, UK: Gower Publishing.

Ortega, R. M., Jose, C., Zuniga, X., & Gutierrez. (1993). Latinos in the United States: A framework for teaching. In D. Schoem, L. Frankel, X. Zuniga, & E. Lewis (Eds.), *Multicultural teaching in the university.* (pp. 51–60). Westport, CT: Praeger.

Orzechowski, R. F. (1995). Factors to consider before introducing active learning into a large, lecture-based course. *Journal of College Science Teaching, 24,* 347–349.

Palmer, P. J. (1998). *The courage to teach: Exploring the inner landscape of a teacher's life*. San Francisco: Jossey-Bass.

Palmer, P. J. (1999). The heart of a teacher: identity and integrity in teaching. *Change, 29*, 14–21.

Pascarella, E. T., Bohr, L., Nora, A., & Terenzini, P. T. (1996). Is differential exposure to college linked to the development of critical thinking? *Research in Higher Education, 37*(2), 159–174.

Perry, W. (1970). *Forms of intellectual and ethical development in the college years.* New York: Holt, Rinehart & Winston.

Pike, B., & Arch, D. (1997). *Dealing with difficult participants*. San Francisco: Jossey-Bass.

Pike, B., & Busse, C. (1995). *101 games for trainers*. Minneapolis: Lakewood Books.

Pintrich, P. R. (1988). In R. E. Young and I. E. Eble (Eds.). College teaching and learning: Preparing for new commitments. *New Directions for Teaching and Learning, 33.* San Francisco: Jossey-Bass.

Pintrich, P. R., Smith, D. A. F., Garcia, T., & McKeachie, W. J. (1991). *A manual for the use of the motivated strategies for learning questionnaire (MSLQ).* The Regents of the University of Michigan.

Reynolds, K. C., & Nunn, C. E. (1998). Engaging freshmen in classroom discussion: Interaction and the instructor techniques that encourage it. *Journal of the First-Year Experience, 10*(2), 7–24.

Richardson, S. M. (Ed.) (1999). Promoting civility: A teaching challenge. *New Directions for Teaching and Learning, 77.*

Rhem, J. (1995). Deep/surface approaches to learning: An introduction. *The National Teaching and Learning Forum, 5*(1), 15–18.

Rickard, H., Rogers, R., Ellis, N., & Beidleman, W. (1988). Some retention, but not enough. *Teaching of Psychology, 15*, 151–152.

Rose, E. (1999). *50 ways to teach your learner.* San Francisco: Jossey-Bass.

Rowe, M. B. (1980). Pausing principles and their effects on reasoning in science. In F. B. Brawer (Ed.), *Teaching in the sciences. New Directions for Community Colleges 31.* San Francisco: Jossey-Bass.

Roth, W. M. (1994). Experimenting in a constructivist high school physics laboratory. *Journal of Research in Science Teaching, 31*(2), 189–223.

Rowe, M. B. (1980). Pausing principles and their effects on reasoning in science. In F. B. Brawer (Ed.), *Teaching in the sciences. New Directions for Community Colleges* 31. San Francisco: Jossey-Bass.

Rubin, L., & Hebert, C. (1998). Model for active learning: Collaborative peer teaching. *College Teaching, 46*(1), 26–30.

Ruhl, K. L., Hughes, C. A., & Schloss, P. J. (1987). Using the pause procedure to enhance lecture recall. *Teacher Education and Special Education, 10,* 14–18.

Samball, K., McDowell, L. (1998). The construction of the hidden curriculum: Messages and meanings in the assessment of student learning. *Assessment & Evaluation in Higher Education, 23*(4), 391–402.

Schapiro, S. R., & Livingston, J. A. (2000). Dynamic self-regulation: The driving force behind academic achievement. *Innovative Higher Education, 25*(1), 23–35.

Schneider, A. (1999, March 26). Taking aim at student incoherence. *The Chronicle of Higher Education,* A16–A18.

Schneider, S. P., & Germann, C. G. (1999). Technical communication on the web: A profile of learners and learning environments. *Technical Communication Quarterly, 8*(1), 37–48.

Schoem, D., Frankel, L., Zuniga, X., & Lewis, E. A. (1993). *Multicultural teaching in the university.* Westport, CT: Praeger.

Seldin, P. (1995). *Improving college teaching.* Bolton, MA: Anker.

Shaluta, C. (2000). *Tech tips.* Retrieved March 9, 2002 from http://www.wku.edu/~shalucp/aug00.html

Shepherd, A., & Cosgriff, B. (1998). Problem-based learning: A bridge between planning education and planning practice. *Journal of Planning Education and Research, 17*(4), 348–357.

Silberman, M. (1995). *101 ways to make training active.* Johannesburg: Pfeiffer and Company.

Silberman, M. (1996). *Active learning: 101 strategies to teach any subject.* Boston: Allyn and Bacon.

Silberman, M. (1998). *Active training*. San Francisco: Jossey-Bass.

Silverman, S. L., & Casazza, M. E. (2000). *Learning and development: Making connections to enhance teaching*. San Francisco: Jossey-Bass.

Simpson, M. L. (1995). Talk throughs: A strategy for encouraging active learning across the content areas. *Journal of Reading, 38*(4), 296–304.

Smith, B. L. (Fall, 1993). Creating learning communities. *Liberal Education,* 32–39.

Smith, K. A. (2000). Getting started: Informal small-group learning in large classes. *New Directions for Teaching and Learning, 82,* 17–24.

Solem, L., & Pike, B. (1997). *50 creative training closers*. San Francisco: Jossey-Bass.

Staley, C. (1999). *Teaching college success*. Belmont, CA: Wadsworth.

Staley, C. C., & Staley, R. S. (1992). *Communicating in business and the professions: The inside word*. Belmont, CA: Wadsworth.

Stearns, S. A. (1994). Steps for active learning of complex concepts. *College Teaching, 42*(3), 107–108.

Stoecker, R. (1990). Strategies for enhancing learning in the "blow-off" course. *Innovative Higher Education, 14*(2), 141–153.

Stocking, S. H., Bender, E. T., Cookman, C. H., Peterson, J. V., & Votaw, R. B. (Eds.). (1998). *More quick hits: Successful strategies by award-winning teachers*. Bloomington, IN: Indiana University Press.

Strom, R. D., & Strom, P. S. (1998). Student participation in the evaluation of cooperative learning. *Community College Journal of Research and Practice, 22,* 265–278.

Sugar, S. (1998). *Games that teach: Experiential activities for reinforcing learning*. San Francisco: Jossey-Bass.

Suskie, L. (2000, May). Fair assessment practices. *AAHE Bulletin*. Retrieved July 26, 2001, from http://www.aahe.org/bulletin/may2.htm

Sutherland, T. E., & Bonwell, C. C. (Eds.). (1996). *Using active learning in college classes*. San Francisco: Jossey-Bass.

Svinicki, M. D., & Dixon, N. M. (1987). The Kolb model modified for classroom activities. *College Teaching, 35*(4), 141–146.

Sylwester, R. (1995). *A celebration of neurons: An educator's guide to the human brain.* Alexandria, VA: Association for Supervision and Curriculum Development.

Tai-Seale, T., & Thompson, S. B. (2000). Assigned conversations. *College Teaching, 48*(1), 15–18.

Terenzini, P. T., & Pascarella, E. T. (1994, January–February). Living with myths: Undergraduate education in America. *Change,* 28–32.

Terenzini, P. T., Pascarella, E. T., & Bliming, G. (1996). Students' out-of-class experiences and their influence on learning and cognitive development: A literature review. *Journal of College Student Development, 37*(2), 149–162.

Thiagarajam, S. T. (1998). *Games that teach.* San Francisco: Jossey-Bass.

Tinto, V. (1987). *Leaving college: Rethinking the causes and cures of student attrition.* Chicago: University of Chicago Press.

Tinto, V. (1988, March). *The principles of effective retention.* Paper presented at the annual meeting of the American Association of Higher Education.

Tinto, V. (1996). Reconstructing the first year of college. *Planning for Higher Education, 25,* 1–6.

Tinto, V. (1997). Classrooms as communities: Exploring the educational character of student persistence. *Journal of Higher Education, 69,* 599–623.

Tinto, V., Goodsell-Love, A., & Russo, P. (1993, Fall). Building community. *Liberal Education,* 16–21.

Upcraft, M., & Gardner, J. (1989). *The freshman year experience: Helping students survive and succeed in college.* San Francisco: Jossey-Bass.

Walvoord, B., & Anderson, V. (1998). *Effective grading.* San Francisco: Jossey-Bass.

Weber, E. (1999). *Student assessment that works.* Boston, MA: Allyn and Bacon.

Weimer, M. (1990). *Improving college teaching.* San Francisco: Jossey-Bass.

Weinert, F. E., & Kluwe, R. H. (1987). *Metacognition, motivation and understanding.* Hillsdale, NJ: Lawrence Erlbaum.

West, E. (1997). *201 icebreakers, group mixers, warm-ups, energizers, and playful activities*. New York: McGraw-Hill.

Whitmire, E. (1998). Development of critical thinking skills: An analysis of academic library experiences and other measures. *College and Research Libraries, 59*(3), 266–273.

Wilkerson, L., & Gijselaers, W. H. (1996). *Bringing problem-based learning to higher education: Theory and practice*. San Francisco: Jossey-Bass.

Will, G. F. (1998, April 13). Disorder in the schools. *Newsweek*, 84.

Wilson, P. (1997). Key factors in the performance and achievement of minority students at the University of Alaska, Fairbanks. *American Indian Quarterly, 21*(3), 535–544.

Wright, W. A.(1995). *Teaching improvement practices : Successful strategies for higher education*. Bolton, MA: Anker.

Zlotkowski, E. (1997). Service learning and the process of academic renewal. *Journal of Public Service & Outreach, 2*(1), 80–87.

Zlotkowski, E. (1998). *Successful service-learning programs: New models of excellence in higher education*. Jaffrey, NH: Anker Publishing Company.